THE WANDERINGS OF A TRAVELING MAN

JIM L. RICHARDSON

THE WANDERINGS OF A TRAVELING MAN

JIM L. RICHARDSON

TABLE OF CONTENTS

ACKNOWLEDGEMENTS

I would like to extend an endearing thanks to Ms. Susan Taft, my friend and editor. She is the lady that I depend on to get the content of my manuscripts laid out in an acceptable fashion. Thank you, Susan.

Also: Thanks to James Winchester, my friend, former student, and graphic designer, for designing the cover of my books and a multitude of other services that make my life much easier. Thank you, James.

DEDICATION

The <u>Wanderings of a Traveling Man</u>, my seventh book, is dedicated to several special friends that I discovered through the journey of my life.

Along with Marjorie Bowles, of the Texas Hill Country, there is Mrs. Ada, up in the Oklahoma Panhandle. Over the years, both ladies and their closest friends and families became family to me.

There are also my many friends in New Mexico, Arizona, Georgia, Mississippi, Louisiana, Arkansas, Kansas, Missouri, Nebraska and Oklahoma that I did not want to leave out.

Dedicated to all of them that opened their doors and took me in as a weary sojourner in a distant land. Every one of them opened their hearts and poured forth their innermost feelings and inspired me to go forward with my offerings.

I could never have found anyone that would have treated me better or so kindly accepted me into their homes and onto their ranches.

Looking back now, the moments spent with these dear souls were some of the happier times of my life. They are only memories now, but they are the type of memories that one carries to their grave.

I started this book with the intent of it containing several individual friends, but as I started writing and recalling such times, I had much more information about certain ones than I could ever imagine.

Maybe in time, I will write a sequel to this offering and list more of those beautiful flowers that I found as I made my journey.

There was never a cross word between any of us during the years that we were close, and I was visiting them regularly. Moments that made days, fell through the hourglass of our lives as we relished every minute of it.

Even until this day, the beginning of hunting season calls my mind away, as I sit and contemplate my wonderful friends from days of old and wish that there was a way to return to those settings once again, even if it were but for a short visit.

Many would call it nostalgia and I would totally agree with them. When thinking about those days, I am overcome with acute nostalgia for those times.

I am asking you to accept these friends just as I have presented them to you; there is a strong possibility of you falling in love with them also.

If you do, I have been successful in illustrating them to you.

Enjoy my wanderings.

Jim L. Richardson

It has been said that the "characters" we write about are those folks that weave their way into our spirits and heartstrings, bringing smiles to our minds as we remember shared experiences with each other and ourselves.

They are a warm spot in our heart that makes an imaginary hug seem minutes old instead of decades ago.

Sometimes, to this very day, when I close my eyes, I can still hear them laughing about making me the prodigal son; what sweet memories they are of my dear friends as they return from time to time to remind me of those days; for those sweet memories, I would take nothing; to relive them one more time, I would give almost anything.

FOREWORD

My gratitude runs deep for the individuals I have met along the pathway of my life. In many instances, I firmly believe that God placed those dear souls along my way.

It is my comfort now, in my later years, to share with each of my readers what I experienced doing what I most loved to do. It all happened too fast.

I invite each of you to meet and get to know these individuals that I hold so dear. In time, maybe you will grow to love them just as I do. If that is obtained, I am more than happy with my work.

Bless you for following my writing, and may God continue to bless us all.

This book, my seventh, <u>The Wanderings of a Traveling Man</u>, will be available in October 2019.

My offerings to date:

<u>From a Duck Blind on Caddo</u>
<u>From a Duck Blind on Caddo Too</u>
<u>From a Duck Blind on Caddo Also</u>
<u>Every Sun That Rises, Brings A New Day</u>
<u>Trail Justice</u> – <u>The Jess Logan Saga</u>
<u>Flowers Along My Way</u>
<u>The Wanderings of a Traveling Man</u>

Feel free to contact me for a personal autographed copy of one or all of them.

PREFACE

This seventh book is titled, <u>The Wanderings of a Traveling Man</u>. It highlights some of the unique individuals that I have crossed paths with during my journey through life.

In some of the relationships, the real meaning of friendship is clearly defined and exemplified. While, in others, underlying messages are quietly brought forth, often discussed and sometimes explained as to their benefit in bonding the particular ties that bound us; some of those closest connections last until this very day.

My stories will take you from the Kiamichi Mountains of Southeastern Oklahoma to the pre-Civil War plantations of Georgia and to the hundreds of empty cartridges and shells that are scattered along the way.

From the beautiful big-bass lakes of Northeast Texas to Walleye on Beaver's Bend.

From the oxbow sloughs of Big Cypress Creek to the flooded flatlands of the Sulphur River and boatloads of catfish and crappie along the way.

From Lake Bistineau to the Grand Lake of the Cherokees, and hundreds of miles of beautiful water in between.

My stories will take you to the crystal-clear streams and rivers of Northern Arkansas and Oklahoma and down the banks of the rivers of Central and South Texas.

The stories will take you to the pristine mountain country of New Mexico to the high plains of West Texas and the Oklahoma and Texas Panhandles.

Some of my stories will bring meat to the pot while others will leave the air full of tail feathers.

Step away from the daily grindstone you are harnessed to and come go with me as we visit the bayous and swamps of South Louisiana and the wonderful fishing and hunting that is found there.

We may take a pirogue down the bayou and slip quietly beneath the Spanish moss as we explore beautiful Caddo and its surrounding waters. We may retrace the passage of the giant paddle wheel steam ships as they made their way through Big Lake, headed toward Jefferson, Texas or New Orleans, La.

On our journeys, you might pause with me at times while we stop and quietly listen to the alluring sounds that we will discover and the wildlife we will encounter at all the different venues.

Close your eyes and let's ride on the back roads to those wonderful places that are hidden away from the major thoroughfares and can only be found by the true cicerones of the modern day.

On such a journey, you will not cease to be amazed as we discover once again, what I have been fortunate in experiencing so many times in the days of my past.

Together, we will discard and overlook the new to find the old and the stories that have been handed down and passed along that defines us. It will be quite the journey, if you are willing to go.

We will break ice once again at the lake's edge on the cold mornings to set our blocks, ahead of the first flight, and patiently wait until it becomes light enough to behold all of the beauty of God's creation as the large greenheads, with wings fully outstretched, softly fall out of the sky and drop in all around us.

It will be the trip that you can later write home about and definitely keep in your memories for the remainder of your life.

I am waiting.

Will you come and go with me?

Some of our desires originate from our own nostalgia and imagination, packed in the same boxes that our loftiest dreams come in.

We choose our own road; yet no one knows whether that is the right road or whether the other path would have led to greater deeds.

MAJORIE TAKES ME HOME

It was dark by now and the near full moon cast a long reflection off the water in the river. We were standing in a perfect position to witness it all, and it was beautiful. I can close my eyes now and relive every moment of it.

"Jim, it is settled; let's go and get your truck. You are spending the night at my ranch, and you will go out in the morning and harvest our supper for tomorrow night. I didn't tell you that I love fried quail," she said.

I said, "Yes ma'am," as I got into her truck.

When we arrived at the home place, I got out of her truck, cranked mine, and followed her about eight miles to her ranch. As I drove down the long ranch road leading up to her beautiful ranch home, little did I know that was the first of many trips up that same road. Some trips would be very happy trips; others, not so much.

But, for tonight, it was an indescribable trip down a road I had never traveled, and it was about to make a drastic change for me.

At the ranch, she told me to get out and put the bird dogs in the barn for the night; she told me to water and feed them there. She also told me to come up to the house when I had finished with the dogs.

As I entered the back door, a lingering smell of dinner hung on the air. Marjorie told me to wash up on the back porch; Juanita had dinner prepared. She would just have to add an extra plate.

I sat down with Marjorie, Walter, her ranch foreman; and Juanita, Marjorie's dear friend, housekeeper and cook.

Marjorie thanked the Lord for His many blessings, and we all dug into a wonderful meal of chicken fried steak, mashed potatoes, brown gravy, hot rolls, corn-on-the-cob and sweet tea.

I have logged many miles all over the country and have never found sweet tea as good as it is made in the Texas Hill Country. That bit of information needed to be added to this story, and I deemed this spot as being the most proper place to mention it to you.

After dinner, Juanita filled my wine glass with a clear dry wine and even though I could not distinguish the taste after I had swirled it a couple of times, it was excellent. After the third glass, I asked, and she said it was from the white grapes that grew on the trellis in the back yard.

As she poured my fourth libation, she told me the sheets had been pulled back on my bed, and it was located down the hall, last door on the right.

The hospitality at my newly-found home was clearly unbelievably inviting.

Juanita was the first one up at four-thirty the next morning, but as soon as the coffee was perking, Marjorie stuck her head in my bedroom door and said it was coffee time. I pulled my jeans and boots on and found my way by following the enticing smell of the coffee.

As I entered the breakfast room, Juanita was pouring Marjorie a cup and reached for another cup for me.

I took the cup and sat down beside Marjorie while she was stirring her coffee and looking as if there was something she was about to ask me.
After a few minutes, it came out, "Jim how was your first night at the ranch and how did you sleep?"

"I do not think that I have ever rested any better," I told her. "I guess it is the clean air and cool nights."

"Clean, Hill Country air, there is none better," she replied to me.

Juanita said she was about to cook breakfast for us and asked me what I wanted.

I told her to bring me exactly what she was preparing for Marjorie. That order for my meal more or less became a joke between us that morning, and I will reveal it at a later point in this book.

Walter came in about that time and said there were two bird dogs that appeared as if they were ready to go hunting this morning. I replied that I knew they were more than ready because they had been cooped up for a couple of days and were getting restless.

He poured a cup of coffee and sat down with the two of us. It was not long until Juanita walked in with the plates lined up on her arm just like the waitresses used to do in the roadside cafés and truck stops. She handed each of us our plate. The fourth one was for her, and she sat down with us for breakfast.

It was the first opportunity that I had to taste prickly pear preserves and let me tell you, they were absolutely delectable.

Her cooking was delicious, and I sure bragged on it. I had nothing but good reasons to brag on it. It was of the quality of food you would find only in the old kitchens.

Juanita and I made friends right off. In me, she had found a man who loved to eat and one that respected the folks that cooked for him.

It was getting near daylight when I had finished my meal, and I told Marjorie I was going out to feed and water my dogs. Then I would be ready to start my hunt.

"When you are ready to start, I will get in my Jeep

and show you where to go," she offered. "There is a grain field down by the river, and I always see a bunch of them down there, in and around the cover and fence rows."

"I will be right back. You have already said enough to get me excited for the day, Marjorie."

Within a few minutes, I returned to the ranch house and announced that I was ready. Marjorie had put on her warm clothes and told me she was going in the Jeep and following me around, so she could watch me hunt. She also said that she had never seen anyone hunt with dogs.

I told her she was in for a real treat.

When we arrived down by the river, Marjorie stopped, and I stopped my truck right behind her. I jumped the dogs out and watched them as they ran around and emptied out to prepare for the day's hunt. It was not but a few minutes until they were ready to start.

When they were finished with their ritual, I motioned for them to move toward the grain fields. There was plenty of stubble cover left to hold birds as they fed. As we moved along up the hill, Marjorie followed behind in her Jeep.

In less than three or four minutes, both dogs froze on solid points, and I was not sure if they were smelling the same covey or not. As stout little wings whirled the partridges to flight, I braced myself and started picking out my shots.

Quail began to fall, and when my gun was empty there were seven of the birds ready to retrieve. The dogs went straight to work to do just that. It only took about two minutes until all the fallen quail were in my hunting jacket.

Marjorie, as excited as I had ever seen anyone, was out of the Jeep and petting the dogs for their great work.

"That beats anything that I have ever seen, the way the dogs worked and how the quail got up and how you dropped them, and how the dogs picked all of them up and brought them to you," and she could have gone on if she hadn't had to stop to catch her breath.

"Marjorie, that is the way it is done back in the Piney Woods. How many do you want for supper?" I asked as I gave her a big smile.

"Twenty-five or thirty will be plenty for the four of us," she said over her shoulder as she turned and returned to her Jeep. She was not going to linger; the north wind was picking up, and it was beginning to bite.

Halfway up the hill, the dogs had four more solid

points, and there were several single shots to fill up the game bag with 35 quail. I called the dogs in, and we returned to the truck. Marjorie had witnessed it all; the embers deep within her had been fanned that morning.

Back at the ranch house, she asked me if I thought she might be able to learn how to shoot the quail.

"Without a doubt," was my answer, "and we can start in the morning if you would like to."

"How about going in to Fredericksburg with me to get some hunting clothes and some bird shot for my 16-gauge and coming back and going after lunch?" was her request to me.

"Marjorie, you are the captain of the ship, and I have just booked passage. Let's go."

She laughed, and we loaded up. She was grinning from ear to ear as we bounced down the long driveway headed out to the main road.

"Jim Richardson, you are a man of instinct," she remarked.

"Instinct you say; I guess you could call it that, my new friend," was my reply to her as she turned west at the main road.

Buck's Outpost had everything we could have possibly wanted to equip Marjorie for her first quail hunt. I complimented her selections and told her that she was fitting for a photograph on the cover of *Outdoor Life*.

That warranted a big laugh, and she obliged as she selected a pair of Browning Upland Game Feather-lite Boots; they set her off perfectly.

"How many shells do I need to buy and what size shot?"

"Let's start with 100 #7½'s."

On the way back to the ranch, I could sense the excitement building in her. When we arrived, she said she was going to have Juanita make us some sandwiches and then we could leave out.

I told her while Juanita was doing that, I would clean the quail I had killed that morning and leave them with Juanita.

In less than one hour, we were in my truck, headed back down to the river, bouncing along, eating tuna fish sandwiches, drinking Coke, and laughing all the way.

MARJORIE'S FIRST QUAIL HUNT

In less than 20 minutes, we were where I had hunted earlier in the day. We stopped and let the dogs out while we loaded our shell bags.

When we finished, we fell in behind the dogs and started hunting across the side of the hill. We had not gone far when I told Marjorie to move on in on the point, raise her gun up and have it ready to get on a quail and pull the trigger.

The covey flushed, Marjorie aimed, Marjorie shot, Marjorie killed her first quail. She was so excited that she dropped her "Sweet-Sixteen" in the stubble and ran to the downed bird. She even beat the dogs to it, and I mentioned to her that she might make a good retriever.

Arriving at the downed quail, she bent over and

picked it up, looked at it at length, placed it within the folds of her hunting jacket, turned to me and smiled bigger than I had ever witnessed anyone smiling.

She walked over and hugged me and said, "thank you for teaching me to quail hunt."

"Marjorie, we need to get one thing straight, I did not teach you to quail hunt. You watched me this morning, and you decided you wanted to do it. You are a natural my friend, and now you are addicted to it," I said as I chuckled under my breath at her.

"When can we start hunting again?" she inquired as she picked up her Browning.

"Whenever you are ready. The dogs are waiting on us and wondering what in the world we are doing."

Marjorie and I started back up the hill, and within 50 yards the dogs were down solid again. I told her that these might be the singles of the covey we just flushed.

Sure enough, one bird whirled its wings and took flight as Marjorie drew another bead and downed it. She yelled out and started her process over again until she realized what she had done and that it was no accident.

Then and there, on the side of that grain stubble hill, Marjorie Bowles became a quail hunter. We finished the hunt that afternoon bagging 21 quail and most of them were dead kills, no wounded.

As we were driving back to the ranch house, I bragged on her prowess with the 16-gauge. As we rode along and laughed about the afternoon hunt and how the dogs had worked, I think at that time we both realized that our paths were meant to cross. The chances for that happening must have been scattered in the stars.

When we entered the ranch house, Juanita met us in the parlor and wanted to know how the hunting went.

"Great," said Marjorie as she began pulling off hunting clothes and telling Juanita all about the afternoon. "I think we have found us a 'keeper,' in more ways than one."

Knowing that Marjorie was referring to me made me happy. I had not been called a 'keeper' in many moons.

"Help me get my boots off, Juanita. They are new and kind of tight, or maybe my feet have swollen during the day," Marjorie said as she sat down, stuck her boot in the air, and waited on Juanita.

Over dinner that evening, there was even more discussion about hunting quail with friends on the ranch. She even mentioned wanting to get up early the next morning and going again; she said she knew another place that we needed to try.

We were up early the next morning drinking coffee and planning our day as Juanita was cooking our breakfast. The hunting day was a repeat of the day before with Marjorie killing almost 50 birds by herself.

By now, she had become relaxed, and the pull on the trigger of her shotgun was getting easier with each shot. Little did she know, but she was fast becoming an upland game bird hunter. I do not think that it bothered her a bit.

The third morning over breakfast, she asked me to find her two trained pointers, so she would have dogs of her own and wouldn't not have to wait until I came down to hunt. She could go anytime she wanted if she had her own dogs.

I agreed that I would get on the phone and see what I could find for her. I mentioned that the current bird season had just started, and the best dogs were in the field.

"We must be careful purchasing bird dogs this time of the year. Some bird dog men are not reputable and will try and unload 'junk' dogs on us at high prices," I warned.

"It would serve us all better if we were to wait until after this season was over and buy our dogs," I continued.

I offered to leave my two dogs with her, but she pitched a fit, saying "no, I will not think about you doing that."

I explained that I had three more dogs at the house that were just as good as the two that she had killed birds over.

"You can keep my dogs and hunt them when you want to, and when I come down to hunt with you, I will leave my dogs at the house," I said as I offered my dogs again.

After much debate, back and forth, she agreed to keep the dogs and promised me several times that they would receive the best of treatment.

"Marjorie, if I had not already known that, I would have never offered to leave them with you in the first place."

She liked that and smiled a long smile at me.

We hunted the next morning until noon. When we came back to the ranch house, I went in and packed for the road home.

There was something very unusual as I hugged and told Juanita and Marjorie goodbye. When I got to Walter, he grinned and shook my hand.

"I will return in two weeks, and we will do it again," I said as I closed the door on my truck.

Marjorie leaned on the downed window and said that she was going to hunt every day until I returned, and each day when she came in from hunting, she was going to set the tub traps.
I gave her a big laugh and told her to start buying freezers; she was going to need them.

As I drove down the long driveway, I looked through my rearview mirror at three friends waving goodbye to me. I thought to myself how nice it would be if I did not have to go back to work in the morning and could just stay and hunt quail with Marjorie. It would have been an extraordinaire life if I could have done it.

JUANITA BAKES ME A CAKE

Thanksgiving Day had come and gone when Marjorie Bowles called me to wish me a happy birthday and to say that Juanita was planning on baking me the delicious coconut cake that I loved and had relished and bragged on several times in the past.

She had asked Marjorie to call me and find out if I had plans for returning before Christmas. Marjorie told me that it would mean a lot to all of them if I would come and be there at the ranch to celebrate my birthday.

It was December 12, 1986, and I had just returned home from the Texas Panhandle where we opened pheasant season and hunted three days in the cold and snow on the grain fields at Sunray, Texas. There was quite a bit of ice, and the birds stuck tight in the cover thus allowing us to be very successful with our hunts. A new little Brittany female that I had gotten out of Edmund, Okla. worked just beautifully setting the birds.

I quickly checked my calendar and told Marjorie that I could be there on December 19 which was two days before my birthday on the 21st. I was slipping up on 39 years and looked forward to returning to my friends, hunting, and enjoying the ranch again.

The day finally arrived for me to leave out and drive down to the ranch. As I was driving, I could not help but think about Juanita's coconut cake and how unique it always was when she made it. Everyone raved about its taste, and much effort went into it to make it so wonderfully delicious.

Juanita absolutely made the best coconut cake I have ever eaten. It was not that coconut cake was my favorite cake, but oh, the way she made it taste. It would take your breath away, and it did so for many years as I returned to Marjorie's ranch.

As I was driving along, it seemed as if the bad cold weather that I endured in the Panhandle a few days ago was following me south. To make it worse, it started raining on me before I got to 281 in Lampasas, and the temperature was noticeably falling. When I arrived in Marble Falls it had worsened to the point that it slowed down all the traffic.

Creeping along, I estimated that I was almost 90 minutes out from reaching the ranch.

At three-thirty in the afternoon, I finally arrived, and Juanita, Walter and Marjorie met me at the truck; they were watching and saw me when I turned off of the main highway. When I cut the engine off in the Suburban, there was a thin and light sleet intermittently falling on my windshield; I had arrived just in time.

After our greetings, I turned to Walter and asked him if he had enough wood laid in for the bad weather that was forecast for the next three days.

He responded that he did and that he had a big stack of dry wood in the barn to mix with the green they had cut on the ranch in October. Dry post oak does make a hot fire because of the density of the wood.

I had loaded two fish cookers before I hit the road south. Walter mentioned to me earlier that he would be castrating calves the first of November and would freeze several plastic tubes of bull testicles for me to prepare one night while I was at the ranch. I had told him that we could plan on a feast, and we could get Marjorie lined up for another big night of entertaining. No one loved entertaining any better than she did.

Walter grabbed my leather traveling bag and carried it to the front porch where he dropped it into a wooden chair. I carried my hanging clothes and Marjorie pulled out my two boot bags from the back seat before we walked together toward the ranch house.

"What night do you want to have your big feed and get-together?" I asked her while we walked along. She told me, "Hush with that kind of talk. You have just arrived and have already started talking about going to work. I will hear no more about it tonight."

Juanita asked about the road conditions and the drive down.

I responded with, "Juanita, it was nearly as bad as any I have ever driven in traveling in this part of the world. The conditions deteriorated quickly as I left the Waco area. A five and a half-hour trip turned into almost nine hours on the road."

"I guess you are starving to death, aren't you?" was her next question.

"Juanita, I am always starving for your cooking and am anxiously awaiting to see what you have prepared us for supper," was my reply to her.

"You will not be disappointed with what you find on our table," she promised me. "I have made Coca-Cola Barbecue Beef Short Ribs with plenty of sauce for us tonight. You remember that Chill Wills recipe that you gave me several years ago? I cooked them on the smoker that you picked out and Mrs. Marjorie bought for us in Fredericksburg a few years back."

"I can almost taste them now. And what about your to-die-for-baked-beans and potato salad that I truly am addicted to?"

She went on to say that she had it all planned for the evening meal and Marjorie remarked that Juanita had been cooking for two days to get ready for my return; the return of the prodigal son.

I walked over to Juanita and gave her a big hug and a peck on the cheek. After that, I did the same to Marjorie and hugged them both together.

"Like my Oklahoma Panhandle friends, you two are fast making the "prodigal" out of me and I love every minute of it," was my statement as I turned them loose with a big smile.

Sometimes, to this very day, when I close my eyes, I can still hear them laughing about making me the prodigal. What sweet memories they are of my dear friends as they return from time to time to remind me of those days; for those sweet memories, I would take nothing. To relive them one more time, I would give almost anything.

As we entered the ranch house, we naturally made our way to the big room and the big fire. It was roaring and had the whole house toasty. It was very receptive as we found ourselves finding a seat while Juanita poured a small libation of Hill Country Sweet Potato Wine.

It was extra dry and just hit the spot perfectly on such a cold afternoon with dear friends. I could not help but think how fortunate I was to have such a place to come and friends to accept me as these dear souls have done.

It was a secluded haven that I had used for many years, and every time I visited the ranch, our bond became stronger. After three or four years, I became part of the family; they all went out of their way to make me feel that way.

In about an hour Juanita called us to dinner. While I had been away, Walter had started courting a lady who lived near the ranch. Her name was Sally Reasoner, and she was a very sweet lady. And, like it should be, she thought Walter was the greatest thing to ever come along. After only a short time around them, I could sense the attraction they had for each other; wedding bells and rice could very well be in their future.

Marjorie said the two had been dating about two months. He had met her one morning at the Dairy Queen in Fredericksburg and yes, she did remind me that I knew what Dairy Queen she was talking about.

Sally had moved to Fredericksburg after her husband had passed away. They had lived in Kansas several years and owned a large packaging company that Sally had sold before moving to Texas.

Sally had been looking for a popular place to set up an antique store and when she did, it was furnished with some really nice antiques. She added a taste of Texas to her inventory as she was always on the lookout for old ranch house antiques.

I could just go in and sit, watch the assortment of different customers file through, and talk with Sally when she had time to visit.

Certain times of the year, Sally found herself busier than she had ever planned. I told her one afternoon in October that she needed to slow down.

I reminded her that she had said over and over that she did not need the money generated by the shop. I went on to tell her to sell the thriving business she had built, marry Walter, and thoroughly enjoy the rest of her life instead of working.

She would only look at me and grin; I knew my advice was worthless to her.

Marjorie had bought several pieces from her, and one morning, after meeting her at the Dairy Queen in Fredericksburg for coffee, Marjorie introduced her to Walter.

Marjorie later told me that she sensed their mutual attraction during that first introduction.

Marjorie also added, "It is the same place that you ran into your old buddy, Bob Phillips, that time when we were in there," she said with a chuckle.

"You will never let me live that one down, will you Marjorie"? I asked. "You set the spurs deep on me with it every time you get a chance."

As I peered at her, she kept laughing and replied, "You have to admit that it was funny, and it is probably funnier today than the day it actually happened. Your reaction when I mention it makes it even funnier now."

Finally, I succumbed to her once again and smiled back as I commented to Juanita that her sweet tea was always one of the highlights of my trip to see them, hoping that would change the subject. It seemed to have worked, for the time being.

She also had homemade bread with her barbecued short ribs, smashed red potatoes, baked beans, fried corn, deviled eggs, spiced apple rings and pickled beets.

When we had finished our dinner, Juanita blessed us with a piece of her cherry pie with her deep and flaky crust that only she could make. It was a top-shelf meal, and everyone bragged on how delicious everything was.

She returned all the compliments with a huge smile and a modest "thank you."

Marjorie and I helped Juanita clear the dining table while Walter and Sally made their way into the big room. After a while, all of us joined them in front of the roaring fire.

It had started getting dark outside, and when I stepped out on the back porch, the snow was beginning to fall on top of the thin coating of sleet; this night could be a doozy. I thought to myself how nice it was to be in a warm ranch house and be back visiting with dear friends.

I glanced at the thermometer that hung on the wall of the back porch, and it read 26 degrees with the barometric pressure still rising. It was going to get colder before morning.

Marjorie asked for another story, and I retrieved one from my things in the bedroom. When I re-entered the big room, Marjorie and Walter were explaining to Sally how reading a story to them was a longtime tradition when I visited.

I sat on the couch next to Marjorie and began with my selection for the night, Linger There.

From partial memory, I read as follows:

LINGER THERE

This November will be twenty-four short years since I took my first stroll along the beautiful Pedernales River. As the subtle stream wandered its lazy way through the Texas Hill Country, its mystique captured a fondness within me that has endured all these years.

Many times, my fishing and hunting expeditions have taken me to picturesque landscapes of majestic mountains, streams and lakes. These grand settings have been wonderful, but none compare to the short and frequent times I have spent on the banks of the Pedernales.

Thanksgiving 1966 was my first visit, and I became enthralled with its beauty. I spent the holidays with a friend and his grandparents on their ranch located in that renowned area.

I have returned at least a dozen times and with each visit my attachment to this part of the world has grown stronger. My planned trips to this locale were always a needed excuse to return and once again behold its splendor. My excuses ranged from going hunting to just visiting old friends. It never really mattered for what reason, as long as I could return and spend some more time there.

When God made the Texas Hill Country, He must have had individuals such as me in mind. He knew the need for a sanctuary where the weary traveler could return, as often as needed, to find a much sought after inner peace and strength to continue on.

I feel as if the time I spend in this part of the world is free time and for those short periods, the sands through the hourglass are momentarily stalled. I have a strange feeling those precious moments are not marked against me as tenure toward my life on earth.

The Hill Country is filled with such colorful ruggedness, and its abundance of wildlife make it quite different from other places I have visited. It takes on its own personality and individuality as it enslaves me with the subtleties of the countryside sprinkled with wildflowers of all colors.

I remember all of them so well and my dear friend Marjorie, who was a neighboring rancher and all the wonderful times that I shared at her place.

Today, many of my old Hill Country friends are gone, and due to other responsibilities, my opportunities to return are not as abundant as they once were; thus, the frequency of my visits are intermittent.

Someday, and I hope not too long, I will return to that wonderful setting of limestone rock and Spanish dagger. With me will be a red-headed little boy who admires his father and like all little boys, wants to be just like his dad.

I have reserved my next visit for him. It will be a special gift from a loving father to a one-day appreciative son. Hopefully, he will behold the magnificence of the land just as I did on my first visit.

If God will permit us, we will stroll along that grand old stream. Together we can enjoy something I have been blessed with for quite some time.

Maybe my son, in time, will kindle a similar love affair with this great land and like myself, enjoy and harbor it in his memories forever.

I want to walk along the river with him and show him how a selected flat rock will skip when thrown just right.

There is a family cemetery in a live oak grove, overlooking the river. There, I want to spend some time and share with him a lesson in Texas history and a deep love of close friends.

I want to take him by Marjorie's ranch and see the array of her wildflowers in the spring. I want to walk with him along the river that runs through her property and show him where Walter and I ambushed the greenheads on a cold morning.

I want him to see it all firsthand and not have to second guess any of the stories I tell him.

Hopefully, one day he will come to understand that it matters not the length of time man has on this earth, but the quality of that allotted time.

Some day when I am gone, perhaps he will return to the Texas Hill Country. Maybe he too can find some of the answers that in time, he will seek.

I pray God will watch over him in my absence and guide him back to some of the places where He guided me and allowed me to find the much-needed solitude.

Perhaps someday he and his son might carry on our tradition and together, enjoy the Hill Country as much as we did.

When they walk along the river and skip stones at twilight, perhaps they will pause, while watching the ripples slowly disappear, and realize that part of me still lingers there.

When I finished, Linger There, I looked up and there was not a dry eye in the room. My semi-recitation had achieved its intended purpose; my writings have always had feelings and emotions hidden between the carefully selected and chosen words I have placed in print.

Sally could not believe what she had just heard and made the statement, "Jim, if you ever put your feelings in a book, I want the first copy."

It saddens me today to know that she did not live long enough to read my work. I waited too long to start publishing my stories. Those dear friends are all gone now and only left me with a multitude of sweet memories. What more could a traveling man ask for?

Marjorie once told me she thought of me as a friend to the world. I look back today and consider the magnitude of her statement; I only wish that it was as true as she believed it to be and that I could live up to those expectations she had for me.

"A Friend to the World," what a tremendous compliment, I thought.

Even years after her death, I remembered her saying that every time I returned to that part of the country. It was just one of those things that I could never completely put away. The thought of it returned many times, and most of the time it was when it was least expected; it was always most welcomed when it did.

It is amazing how something said or done cuts its place deep into the stone walls of the canyons of your mind.

About ten-thirty, we all turned in for the night with Sally sleeping in the guest bedroom and Walter returning to the bunkhouse. On his way out the door, Juanita reminded everyone that breakfast might be a little later in the morning.

I had heard her say that several times in the past, but I never remember her having it ready later than the normal time. The normal time was about daylight.

Sure enough, when I made it to her kitchen at five, the coffee pot had just finished perking and she was placing the cups on the table.

"Come and get you a cup, my friend, and may I be the first to wish you a great 39th birthday."

"Thank you so much, my dear friend," I said as I poured myself a cup of her hot coffee.

About the same time as I poured the steaming cup and sat down, Marjorie and Sally came into the dining area. It would not be long until Walter would walk through the door.

In a few moments, Walter entered the back door and joined us at the table.
"Twenty-two degrees and it will fall another four or five at sun up," he said as he sat down.

"What makes that, Walter?" was my question to him concerning his statement.

He said, "Jim, I do not know why it is that way, but it has been as long as I can remember."

"And I agree, Walter, but I have never found anyone who could explain to me what caused the temperature to drop like that at daylight. I asked a meteorologist one night in Ft. Worth and all he had was a long answer with no information. After listening to him go through his long explanation, I think I knew less than I did before I asked him."

After sausage, hot biscuits, brown gravy, scrambled eggs, orange marmalade, fig preserves from the trees in the garden, churned butter, and cold milk, we helped Juanita straighten up the kitchen and dining area.

Walter and I walked out on the back porch for him to light his pipe and when we did, there was a large flight of greenheads that fell out of the sky and glided to the quiet water behind the bend in the Pedernales. It had to be frozen but that is exactly where they went down.

"It is just a few feet away from where we built the new bridge several years ago." Walter said.

"Jim, do you want me to drive you down that way and let you ambush them like you did one time before?"

"I don't think so, Walter. It is cold, the wind is picking up, and I am not as mad at them this morning as I have been in the past. Let's let them rest in the bend and eat the abundant live oak acorns."

"Let's go and gather up some wood for the fire, fill the fire box, and just take it easy," he said. "You know it is your birthday, right?"

"Yes, I remember well because Juanita mentioned it to me first thing, and then Marjorie and Sally wished me well on my big day. To tell you the truth, I am waiting on that big coconut cake that

Juanita is going to surprise me with. She has not mentioned it since I arrived, but she always prepares one for me."

Dry wood from the barn, and not so dry wood from the rack, filled the fireplace, the fire box, and we made a big stack on the back porch; it was going to be one of those "feed the fire" kind of days. I could not think of a better way of relaxing and enjoying the peace of a snowy day in the Texas Hill Country.

It was about mid-morning when I heard Juanita mention that she must get started on my birthday cake. As she sauntered into the kitchen, Marjorie asked her if she needed anything or any help making it.

"Ms. Marjorie, I appreciate you offering to help me but there is no need. I have it under control and being that I have made it so many times before, I can almost make it from memory."

"I want to get it made before lunch and let it sit until after dinner. It tastes much better after it sits for at least four hours. It even tastes better the next day and the day after that." Juanita added.

She went on to explain how the tastes would meld together after it rested for a few days.

JUANITA'S COCONUT CAKE

Ingredients:

$3/_4$ pound (3 sticks) unsalted butter, at room temperature, plus more for greasing the pans
2 cups sugar
5 extra-large eggs, at room temperature
$1^1/_2$ teaspoons pure vanilla extract
$1^1/_2$ teaspoons pure almond extract
3 cups all-purpose flour, plus more for dusting the pans
1 teaspoon baking powder
$1/_2$ teaspoon baking soda
$1/_2$ teaspoon kosher salt
1 cup milk
4 ounces sweetened shredded coconut

For the frosting:

1-pound cream cheese, at room temperature
$1/_2$ pound (2 sticks) unsalted butter, at room temperature
$3/_4$ teaspoon pure vanilla extract
$1/_4$ teaspoon pure almond extract
1-pound confectioners' sugar, sifted
6 ounces sweetened shredded coconut

Directions:

Preheat the oven to 350 degrees F. Grease 2 (9-inch) round cake pans, then line them parchment paper. Grease them again and dust lightly with flour.

In the bowl of an electric mixer fitted with a paddle attachment, cream the butter and sugar on medium-high speed for 3 to 5 minutes, until light yellow and fluffy.

Crack the eggs into a small bowl. With the mixer on medium speed, add the eggs 1 at a time, scraping down the bowl once during mixing. Add the vanilla and almond extracts and mix well. The mixture might look curdled; don't be concerned.

In a separate bowl, sift together the flour, baking powder, baking soda and salt. With the mixer on low speed, alternately add the dry ingredients and the milk to the batter in 3 parts, beginning and ending with dry ingredients. Mix until just combined. Fold in the 4 ounces of coconut with a rubber spatula.

Pour the batter evenly into the two pans and smooth the top with a knife. Bake in the center of the oven for 45 to 55 minutes, until the tops are browned, and a cake tester comes out clean. Cool on a baking rack for 30 minutes, then turn the cakes out onto a baking rack to finish cooling.

For the frosting, in the bowl of an electric mixer fitted with a paddle attachment, combine the cream cheese, butter, vanilla and almond extract on low speed. Add the confectioners' sugar and mix until just smooth (don't whip!).

To assemble, place 1 layer on a flat serving plate, top side down, and spread with frosting. Place the second layer on top, top side up, and frost the top and sides. To decorate the cake, sprinkle the top with coconut and lightly press more coconut onto the sides. Serve at room temperature.

About ten o'clock that morning, the beautiful cake was finished and was placed on a turntable pedestal that sat in the middle of the dining table. It was so inviting, and I do not think that I have ever seen a professionally made cake that was any prettier.

When I told Juanita the same, she only smiled and thanked me for my compliment.

"How many years have you been coming to the ranch?" she asked me as a solemn look fell across her face.

"Juanita, this season is the ninth year that I have been down here to hunt and to see all of you," was my answer.

"It sure does not seem that long that you have been coming down," she replied as she turned to go back into the kitchen.

Marjorie was just sitting and listening to our conversation without saying anything.

Eventually, she remarked, "I cannot get over all of the wonderful times that we have shared since you have been coming."

After a while, she said, "Jim, come and go with me to the feed store in Blanco. We need to get some grain for the wildlife. This snow cover makes it tough on them."

After bundling up, we both got into her Jeep, hooked to the trailer, and I drove her to town. Once there, we loaded the small trailer with milo and corn chops and headed back to the ranch house.

On our way back to her ranch, the wind blew harder, and she reached over and turned the heater on full blow.

She looked at me and remarked, "As you get older it is harder to stay warm on a cold day. In time, you will know what I am talking about."

When we arrived, we saw Walter with the John Deere cab tractor and grain blower loaded with milo; he had the same idea as did we, in feeding the wildlife.

The beauty of the grain blower was it could be directed to blow the feed exactly where you wanted it. It was ideal for blowing around and under the chaparral, "shinnery," and other scrub oak brush on the fence rows between the grain plots.

The twisted undergrowth was so thick that there was very little snow accumulation in those spots and the quail and other birds could find cover and feed together.

Marjorie told me to drive down by the river and we would put our grain out under the huge live oaks for the turkeys. The live oaks were so thick that they had bare ground under them that made a great location for the turkey to come and eat.

While the ground was covered in snow, most of the turkeys were roosting in the live oaks and our grain placement was very convenient for them.

After we scattered the corn chops and milo, we drove back up on the edge of a nearby knoll and watched a multitude of turkeys descend from the trees and start feeding under the live oaks.

It was a good feeling that came over me while watching them eat. I told Marjorie about the feeling that I had just experienced. Those feelings were kind of chilling to me.

She looked at me and smiled while saying, "Jim, I know the feeling and that is why I do it. That is the reason I put the grain out for them when the conditions are like this."

The third afternoon at the ranch, everyone decided it was time for me to cook up the calf fries. I had done it for them twice before, and it was quite an ordeal as the stakeholders stood around and watched me prep the fries and get them ready for the hot grease.

The weather had let up a bit and Marjorie decided that she would invite several of her closest friends and neighboring ranchers to the shindig; most of those Hill Country neighbors had eaten them before or at least had heard of them.

Several of our guests had been at the previous two dinners when calf fries were served and liked them to the point of coming back for some more.

Walter donned a chef's apron, and Sally placed a large chef's hat on his head and folded it down toward the right front of his head. It was kind of comical to those of us that knew him well.

It was almost by the time I removed the calf fries from the freezer and shucked them down without the membrane, that most of our invited guests had arrived and were enjoying cocktails from the bar area that was being run by a bartender from a not-so-nearby Holiday Inn Club.

Marjorie had hired him to serve drinks and to entertain along with the neighboring lady rancher violin player from the San Antonio social circuit. Her fiddle playing could sure set the mood for an enjoyable evening. I would have loved to have heard her break it down in a honky-tonk.

During all the carrying on, Marjorie had broken out her fancy drinking glasses with the short stem on them. The professional wait staff that she had serving the event made it a point to keep everyone's glass filled to the brim.

She had a knack for always doing everything first class, and this time was no different; she was a natural when it came to entertaining. She was great at moving through and working a gathering of people to see that everyone's needs were being met.

Like in the past, the first thing I did was to cull Marjorie's fancy glassware and replace it with a wide-mouth quart Mason jar from the kitchen. I kept it on a nearby stump in close proximity of where I was working, and the servers had no trouble in finding it and keeping it brimming.

About half of the group, with cocktails in hand, eased over to the cutting block where I was working, preparing the calf fries.

While prepping the fries, about three gallon of crinkle-cut French fries were added to the boiling grease. They went to rolling, and it was not long until they rattled like bones when they were stirred with a wire spatula.

Once the potatoes were removed from the grease and placed on paper towels in grocery store brown paper sacks and the tops were rolled closed to keep the heat in, the calf fries were called for.

When they were coated and covered completely with the flour and cornmeal, they were individually dropped into a cast iron wash pot of 375-degree cottonseed oil that Walter had secured for just the occasion.

The calf fries were a sight to behold as they rolled in the boiling grease and gradually started turning golden brown.

I told the story of how Chill Wills called them scallops when I was cooking them for Mrs. Enid Justin's gathering at the Ft. Worth Stock Show and Rodeo one year.

When they were finished, they were poured out on a large serving platter and the sacks of crinkle-cut fries were poured beside them.

Juanita had coleslaw, pickled beets and peaches to serve along with them. There was a bowl full of a special "fire and ice" pickle relish to have as another condiment that proved to be a hit with the crowd. There were four gallons of Sweet Hill Country Tea for those that were not drinking cocktails.

For her desserts, Juanita brought out eight of the most beautiful lemon ice-box pies that she had made for the occasion. The whipped peaks were golden on their tops and when the meal was complete, there were two slices left of one pie. They had been thoroughly scarfed up by the guests.

The crowd grew quiet as everyone served themselves and took a seat at the long dining table. We had done it again; we had placed a superb meal in front of our visitors.

Often, I think about what I would give for just one more afternoon, one more opportunity to drive back down and return to Juanita's table with my friends. I would want everything to be just as I had left it when I last visited there.

If I could return, I would definitely look for those two remaining pieces of her lemon pie. I have never had lemon pie so good.

MY CALF FRIES

Ingredients:

12 calf fries (3 pounds) with membrane attached
1 cup milk
1 egg
$1^1/_2$ cup all-purpose flour
¾ cup cornmeal
$1^1/_2$ teaspoons salt
½ teaspoon pepper
Vegetable oil

How to Prepare Them:

Place calf fries with membranes on a baking sheet, and freeze.

Slit each membrane; pull away from calf fries, and discard. Slice calf fries cross-sectional into thick strips of about ½ inch.

Combine milk, egg, and two shakes of Louisiana Hot Sauce in a medium mixing bowl, beating well. Add calf fries, and soak 1 hour.

Drain, discarding milk mixture.

Combine flour, cornmeal, salt, and pepper; dredge in flour mixture, and fry in deep, hot oil (375°) or until golden brown.

Drain well on paper towels and serve hot.

Whenever and wherever I prepared my calf fries, I made a highly addictive dipping sauce to go with them.

Every time these "fixings" were prepared, we got nothing but rave reviews from our guests.

PRAIRIE NUGGET
AND MOUNTAIN SCALLOP DIPPING SAUCE

Ingredients:

1 cup mayonnaise (I prefer Hellman's or Dukes)
½ cup Heinz ketchup
1 tablespoon Worcestershire sauce plus 1
    teaspoon

1 teaspoon garlic powder
1/4 teaspoon salt
1 teaspoon Accent
½ teaspoon chili powder (Gebhardt)
1 teaspoon black pepper (fresh ground is best)

Instructions:

In a small bowl combine all ingredients and mix until well blended.

Store in an air-tight container for a few hours before serving.

Will stay good in a container for up to two weeks.

Yields: $1^1/_2$ cups

An old West Texas agriculture teacher friend of mine taught me how to prepare the calf fires this way, and I am often reminded of the cold afternoon and night I cooked them for a large group out at the Ft. Worth Stock Show and Rodeo Fairgrounds. The year was about 1975.

It happened to be during the time that I met Chill Wills and Will Geer. They were also staying out on the west side of Ft. Worth at Kahler Green Oaks Inn. We were all in town for the special occasion, and I invited both of them to the cookout.

I was living and breathing first class all the way since Mrs. Enid Justin had allowed me to stay in her personal suite. I later found that she had special interests in the establishment and whatever she asked for seemed to happen quickly. Such was the case of my accommodations during my visit.

That was also the year that Chill Wills gave me his Coca-Cola barbecue sauce recipe. It was just a couple of years before Mr. Wills passed away. He was a native of Seagoville, Texas. I will share that recipe with you before we leave Chill.

Mrs. Enid Justin of Nocona Boot Company fame, who I had gotten to know several years prior, asked me to prepare my calf fry recipe for a large gathering that she had planned. She requested that I cook up an equal portion of chicken nuggets and crinkle cut fries to go along with the calf fries. She furnished everything, along with two of her gourmet chefs to assist me in the preparation of the meal.

Surveying her guests, I do not remember ever seeing as many diamonds, pearls, expensive western outfits on both men and women, white 20X beaver Stetsons, gold belt buckles and turquoise jewelry.

"Extremely fancy" are the only words that I can think of to describe the carryings-on; maybe too fancy to be waiting around to eat calf fries, I thought to myself.

I do not think there was a fur-bearing animal left in all of North Texas. Their pelts had been harvested and were all donned by these guests.

I wore my snake skin items that Tony from the Oklahoma Panhandle ranch had made me. Many compliments were passed my way and several inquiries as to where I purchased such perfect craftsmanship.

I wish that I had had enough time to tell them the whole story, about Mrs. Ada and her ranch up in the Panhandle, and the others that lived there; however, the hot peanut oil would not allow me that time. I had to get busy; maybe I could tell them later.

I felt good about the way I looked with all the dignitaries at the gathering. I knew, and most of them knew, by comparison, I had not "come in barefoot."

The last time I had seen such a crowd was during the awards ceremony after the big cutting show in December. I have never seen as many beautiful Texas women in one spot in all my life. There is no place in the world like Ft. Worth during the cutting show.

I had a dear friend who used to say, "We are only in town for the cutting; when it is over, we will be gone."

The bar was open, and the ladies and gentlemen were greasing their cogs as Mrs. Enid's chefs brought out the near frozen calf fries and started prepping them.

Several asked if I had brought a bunch of Pittsburg Hot Links to the affair. I grinned at Mrs. Enid and remarked that what I had was better than any hot links. I heard her chuckle as she walked away from the preparation table.

Many of the guests were standing around the cheese table, whittling on a variety of cheese rounds and different kinds of crackers. As the cocktails flowed, there were plenty of those high-falutin' tales being told.

The alcohol had whetted their appetites and now there were more of them, with cocktails in hand, moving in our direction.

We had two large flat stainless-steel pans that were about eight inches deep, four foot by six foot with four inches of peanut oil that was almost ready to ignite the floating wooden match to show that the temperature for frying had been reached.

Most of the watchful attendees marveled how the hot grease could ignite the floating match; some had never seen that trick before.

We placed chicken nuggets in one pan along with the prepped calf fries. The chicken nuggets were coated the same as the calf fries.

Mr. Wills stood next to the cooking pans with a glass of ice cubes and about three fingers of his favorite bourbon poured over them. He told jokes and kept everyone entertained while we finished up the meal; his voice carried all over the show barn and attracted some that were not even invited.

Mrs. Enid did not care. She would have fed Ft. Worth and probably could have afforded it. What a darling soul she was.

As the fries and nuggets were rolling in the cooking pan, we placed crinkle cut French fries in the remaining pan and got them going the same way.

Chill started calling the calf fries scallops and assured everyone within ear shot that they were not going to be disappointed with this meal and that they would be coming back for seconds.

As everything finished up about the same time, it was all removed from the hot grease and placed on racks for a couple of minutes to drain.

As we replenished the cook pans with more scallops, nuggets, and French fries, Mrs. Enid quietened the crowd, asked the blessing, and turned everyone loose on the prepared food and all the trimmings to go with it. There was coleslaw, deviled eggs, spiced apple rings and an assortment of pickles.

When the first batch was plated up, the second batch was placed on the draining racks. The flow through the line was continuous until everyone had their fill.

As the food was consumed, Mrs. Enid was more than happy with the response of her guests. Most of them came by and gave her a personal "thank you" for her kindness.

Chill stood up and told everyone that he was so appreciative of Mrs. Enid and to buy her boots every time they got the chance.

He followed that with, "Y'all follow me over to the Round-Up Inn and listen to some really good fiddle music tonight and maybe some of us can two-step a bit."

When it was over, and we were cleaning up, Mrs. Enid came over and asked me if I would come to Nocona in April and cook for another event similar to this one except it would be for her employees. Without hesitation, I told her to count me in; once the date was set, I would mark it on my calendar.

Before the night was over, I got a chance to tell several stories about Mrs. Ada and her Oklahoma Panhandle ranch.

The story of my failings in the bird dog breeding and quail hunting world was more than evident in my story of Trouble. After all these years, I still cringe when I think of some of his capers; there will never be another one like him.

TROUBLE

Trouble has come to us, many times, unexpected. Sometimes it comes right out of the blue with no prior warning. Many times, after its arrival we look back and realize that some of it was of our own doing.

Not the case with my Trouble. My Trouble was a six-week old puppy that a dear friend, on the plains of Northeast Oklahoma, gave to me as a present some thirty-five years ago.

My Trouble was a black and white English pointer with superb lineage. He was papered under the name of Gun Smoke's Last Stand. His paternity bloodline traced back to the original Gun Smoke and from a fine Elhew female.

A good bird dog man could look at his pedigree and determine quickly that Trouble would develop in to a successful hunting dog.

Much time and energy were devoted, at an early age, to develop him into a first-class hunter. When it came time to break him to heel, it came naturally. When he was old enough, he was forced broke to retrieve on the handler's table. Trouble responded well to everything he was asked to do.

Field trialing friends and acquaintances of mine who saw Trouble run all asked for the opportunity to add him to their strings. There was no doubt in my mind about having a champion.

Trouble grew into a medium size dog that had ground burning speed. He had a 12 o'clock tail that worked straight up and clockwise while he was running.

When standing and admiring him work it was easy to think that he might be one of the best that was ever put down.

My thoughts afield would run wild as the young prospect was envisioned burning ground over great bird cover in numerous places. From the plains of Nebraska to the plantation hunts in Georgia and a hundred places in between would be his domain. All he had to do was to do his part which should only come natural to him.

The first sign of a problem was with the difficulty of keeping him in a pen. Special efforts had to be taken to build a pen that would secure him. He was a climber, a jumper, and a digger, among other things.

All of those were big negatives but his looks, breeding, and style more than made up for those imperfections.

I began hunting Trouble in a brace with a seasoned hunting dog. At first, he seemed to manage, but as he matured he wanted no part of hunting with another dog or honoring him afield.

It was a full-time job to work with him on breaking bad habits when I had no idea of their origin.

It was finally decided that he would be hunted by himself.

This worked fairly well until Trouble decided he would range farther and farther away. He found quail and a lot of them, but he would bust coveys and not hold points until the hunter arrived.

It was very disappointing to see this perfect specimen of a hunting dog totally going to pieces.

He became completely worthless to a hunter on foot. Field trialing was my next option for him. Two different trialers took him and worked with him for a short time. They returned him just shaking their heads and said that he ranged too far and would not heed their commands.

One of my old field trialing bird dog friends from Kansas heard about Trouble, heard about my predicament, and gave me a call.

He told me that he would take Trouble and finish him out. He also said that he had been looking for a wide-ranging dog to add to his string. Little did he know, at that time, he had found just that, a wide-ranging dog. It made me smile when he told me.

We met in Big Cabin, Oklahoma, and he took possession of my wide-ranging pointer. Trouble was bigger and healthier now than he had ever been. The other two handlers had him dragging log chains to slow him down. That only built him up more and made him stronger. He was more prepared for the Iditarod than field trialing.

Trouble lasted two months with my Kansas friend.

Trouble was dropped off to me as they traveled to training grounds in South Texas. Trouble almost ended our friendship of many years.

Hard headed, he was called by my friend. The previous two handlers had gone farther than that.

Trouble was back at home at Gun Hill Kennel and looked like that was where he was going to stay. Every time he came to my mind, sadness would overtake me thinking about such a beautiful specimen and how useless he was to me as a hunting dog.

Mrs. Ada, up in the Oklahoma Panhandle, called Christmas Eve and invited me and another friend to come to her ranch and hunt quail during the first week of January.

When we packed our gear, and left for the trip we took Trouble, along with three other dogs with us.

There was an idea in the back of my mind that we might have found a new home for him. I knew how Mrs. Ada loved English Pointers, especially black and white ones. She would not care about his hunting ability because she would make a pet out of him.

We arrived at her ranch late on a Sunday afternoon, and upon arrival we met her at her stately ranch house. She greeted us, as in the past, in her usual abundant hospitable way.

Her ranch was like a second home to me as I had visited her many times on different hunts. Thanksgiving had been spent with her on two different occasions through the years, and she always treated me as part of her family.

During the evening meal Mrs. Ada was told of my trials and tribulations with Trouble.

As soon as breakfast was over on the following morning, Mrs. Ada met us at the truck. We were feeding and watering our dogs, and she immediately recognized the black and white pointer we had spoken of. She went over to him, petted him on the head, and the attraction for the two of them was easily recognizable.

Trouble was left with her when we loaded up to start the hunt. As we drove out of her yard I looked back through my rear-view mirror and Mrs. Ada and Trouble were headed through the front door of the ranch house.

We had a very successful morning hunt, and when we came in for lunch I stopped at the water spigot at the windmill trough in the yard and cleaned 30 quail for supper. Upon entering the kitchen, the birds were handed to Juanita to put on ice.

When entering the big room, there was Mrs. Ada

sitting in her lounge chair by the fireplace and Trouble was stretched out, upon her big couch, enjoying the fire.

Mrs. Ada said that they had spent the morning getting acquainted, and I knew at that time that the deal was done.

They had taken the Kubota and rode down to the working pens where her men were separating replacement heifers. After that they rode several miles out on the range to check two other herds. She said Trouble loved riding on the front seat with her and had acted like he had been doing it for years.

After a short lunch, we went back afield for an afternoon hunt. Quail were plentiful that year, and we were very successful.

For dinner we had fried quail, white skillet gravy from the drippings, and cat head biscuits. There was fried corn fresh off the cob, mashed potatoes, and a sweet potato pie made from the bushel of potatoes that we had brought her. Two of Mrs. Ada's sisters joined us for the meal.

Juanita had cooked the meal for us as she had cooked meals for Mrs. Ada for over forty years, and her cooking was magnificent. Gourmet chefs could not compare with her expertise.

After the meal, we retired to the big room and opened a bottle of her best homemade brandy. It was a cold night outside and the fireplace was rolling. The brandy hit the spot and the fiddle music filled the old ranch house.

Trouble was still on the couch. He did not even want to go to the truck for his evening meal. I made the remark that "Sorry" would have to become his middle name.

Later we learned that he had been snacking on treats most of the afternoon. Mrs. Ada had a way of capturing his heart. He had never been treated so well.

After four days of hunting, eating and entertainment, we started making preparations to return home.

As in the past, it was hard to leave this kind of hospitality and the quality of quail hunting that we had once again, enjoyed.

It was Friday afternoon when we told Mrs. Ada goodbye. She never mentioned keeping Trouble. She had already decided on that.

As we loaded and started down the long driveway between the large live oaks I looked at my friend, winked, and said "mission accomplished."

Trouble now had miles and miles of open range with no barb wire. He could range as wide as he wanted. He could run and hunt on his own. We knew that we had found a special place for him.

Upon a return two years later to Mrs. Ada's ranch, we were told that Trouble hardly ever left the ranch house unless he was riding in the Kubota with Mrs. Ada. Their friendship only grew stronger through the years.

It was reported by the ranch hands that Trouble was observed from time to time, in the front yard, under the live oaks, with a covey pointed.

About a month after arriving back home, Mrs. Enid called one night and asked me what size boot I wore. In three weeks, two of the prettiest pair of goat skin round toe cowboy boots arrived in the mail. One pair was a grey and the other was a dark blue. They looked great with Wranglers.

When I arrived in Nocona the first of April, I expressed my thanks to her. I did love Mrs. Enid and told her that I had done her cookouts because of her and the lady that she was, and that I had expected nothing of monetary value from her.

She looked at me for a long time and finally replied, "I know, Jim. I know. I just wanted to. You can at least allow an old woman her happiness. Giving you those boots made me happy."

I gave her a long hug and thanked her for her generosity. She just smiled and hugged me back. Gosh, I was looking forward to spending a few days on her ranch in Nocona.

I had a ball, riding and roping with the ranch hands and getting to know each of them. We spent the second day separating and weaning calves from their mothers and driving them down to the working pens.

Upon arrival, the whole bunch was worked and branded with a rocking N on their hips. Many of the ranch hands had been with Mrs. Enid for several years and were very faithful to her spread.

On that trip to her ranch I first heard the expression "ride for the brand" from one of her cowboys, and it has stuck with me since the day that I heard him say it.

It is all about loyalty and dedication to an employer, and her cowboys were dedicated; she took the best of care of them and their families and they appreciated it.

There is nothing like being part of a family. The love, trust, and dedication between family is unexplainable.

I will not leave this part without finishing with Chill Wills and his recipes that he shared with me.

CHILL WILLS' COCA-COLA BARBECUE

Ingredients:

2 cups Coca-Cola (or similar cola)
2 cups ketchup
$1/_2$ cup white vinegar
$1/_2$ large onion, finely chopped
1 tablespoon black pepper
$1/_4$ cup brown sugar
3 tablespoons salt
3 tablespoons chili powder

The famous Chill Wills (movie star) cooked barbecue brisket at the Ft. Worth Livestock Show and Rodeo back in 1976 and used this Coca-Cola sauce on it.

When I asked him for his recipe he just handed me another drink that he was mixing. Later that night, when it had quietened down considerably, he walked over to where I was and handed me my own copy and it was signed, from your friend, Theodore Childress "Chill" Wills.

I have kept the recipe with his signature on it and have cherished it down through the years. From time to time, I have shared the same recipe in my stories along the way.

I know he would be proud of me remembering him in this way.

I can close my eyes and still see him standing there, preparing the recipe, while singing, *I'm Just a Coca-Cola Cowboy*, and that would garnish other laughter from afar.

.   .   .

The employee cook-out at Mrs. Enid's ranch in Nocona was really nice. She had everyone there that worked at her boot manufacturing facility and a representative from most of her suppliers.

Surprisingly, I ran into my dear college friend, Steve Jernigan, who managed Cutter Bill's Western World at the Galleria in Houston. I had not seen him in about ten years, and we were both really surprised to see each other again.

As we visited, he shared with me that The Nocona Boot Company had helped put Cutter Bill's Western World on the map in Houston, Texas. He also said that he had bought from Mrs. Enid for several years, and they had become close friends. He had many wonderful things to say about their friendship.

I told him about the big shindig in Ft. Worth that she had sponsored and how I had cooked the meal for her.

Steve looked at me, shook his head, and said, "It is such a small world, my friend, isn't it?"

We both laughed, and he agreed to stay a couple of extra days so that we might catch up on what we had missed the last few years. Steve had been a "chick magnet" at North Texas State and was a good man to hang out with if you loved the women.

He was a local Denton High School student when I first met him, and we became friends immediately. We kept the high school student story a secret, and all of the college girls both at North Texas and TWU thought he was much older.

Steve and I lived together for two years in an apartment that was just across the street from Texas Woman's University. There were pool parties every weekend and apartment parties every night around the complex.

If that was not enough excitement, Jessie Lopez, brother of Trini Lopez, and his band also lived in the complex. It was not uncommon for them to hold pool jam practice sessions on Sunday afternoon.

Steve's family owned a ranch south of Denton, just east of IH 35 South. We had many parties out there when we weren't partying at our apartments just off the TWU campus.

Well anyway, Steve and I got a chance to visit during the two days that he stayed on the ranch with me. One afternoon we took an old Volkswagen dune buggy and drove up on some cliffs overlooking the Red River. There, we just sat and drank cold beer, discussing the water that had passed under our bridges since we had last seen each other; sometimes reminiscing about old times and old friends is heart touching.

For several hours, we revisited those many carefree days that we had spent as young adults, with very little responsibility.

We relived the days in North Austin and at Threadgill's with Janis Joplin, before her hook-up with the California Connection and eventually her demise. The memories were wildly thrown around, and names of friends mentioned brought back a world of old memories that had almost been forgotten.

We talked about when we first floated the Guadalupe River and all the fun and wild experiences we had there with other young friends.

After three days, Steve left out after telling us all goodbye, and other than his voice on a distant phone connection, we have had very little contact through the years. The loops that each of us built after that never seemed to intertwine again; it is really a shame considering how close we once were and the many precious moments we once shared.

This rambling venture was entertaining, but it is time to get back to Marjorie, Juanita, Walter and Sally, down in the Texas Hill Country.

The older I get the easier it is for me to get sidetracked. Sometimes the thoughts of the beauty I find in those distractions linger in my mind for quite some time. Often times, they even offer me more kindling for my stories from my past.

.   .   .

Marjorie had bought me a new white Stetson for a birthday present and she always received a great pleasure in presenting her presents to me. Once again, I told her that she should not have bought me a thing.

"Allowing me to come and visit, hunt on your ranch and enjoy all of the hospitality that all of you offer is ample reward for me," as I continued.

Marjorie loved to surprise people and I think that the hat was bought for me as a big surprise more than anything else. Regardless, it was a beauty and she knew that I loved white hats. It was from Coker's in Ft. Worth, and she had made a special trip up that way to pick it out.

Her remark to me when she handed me the box was, "Only good guys wear white and you have always been a good guy."

After presenting me with the hat, she had an additional surprise for me. Another box from Montana Silversmiths held a beautiful buckle with gold and silver trim. It was absolutely gorgeous, and I wasted no time replacing it for the silver buckle that I was wearing.

Come to find out, everyone had chipped in on the belt buckle and Marjorie had special ordered it just for me. I never found out what they paid for it, but I do know that they are not given away.

They did remember my birthday and were determined that I was at the ranch for the presentation of what they had bought me.

Occasionally, even today, I pause and mentally look back at the wonderful people that I had made dear friends with and wonder how in the world could I have been so lucky; God must have had a hand in it.

The second night after I arrived at the ranch, the driving snow and the unexpected bad spell knocked out the power supply from the Pedernales Electric Cooperative, and we were forced to break out the coal oil lamps.

Early the next morning, Walter and I went down to the barn and attempted to start the diesel generator that had not been used in several years.

After several attempts and much careful observation, it was decided that the carburetor had to have a rebuild.

We disassembled it and thoroughly cleaned it but to no avail. We had to go into town and get the kit required to do the rebuild.

Marjorie fired up the Suburban with the four-wheel drive and we hit the road toward Fredericksburg. When we arrived, we found the parts store and luckily, they had our kit in stock. Upon leaving the auto store, we drove by the Dairy Queen on the way back to Marjorie's.

I just sat in the passenger side seat and waited for her to make some remark about our past experience in there. Surprisingly, after several minutes, nothing was said as she pointed the Suburban home and moved along at a steady clip.

Upon arrival back at the ranch, she instructed Walter to get one of the ranch hands to fill the generator tank with diesel. It held fifty gallons and would run the big 40,000 KW for two full days.

Walter had talked a drilling field supervisor from a big oil company out of it several years ago when they were drilling the shallow wells around in the area. They had it delivered to the ranch and the supervisor even sent a company electrician over to install it and hook it up to the main line to supply electricity with the flip of a lever.

"I told you when we got that thing that we would rely on it from time to time when we lost our electrical service," was his reminder to all that securing the generator was his idea.

Walter and I went to work on the carburetor rebuild, and in about an hour we had it all put back together. In the meantime, the battery had been charging. When Walter hit the switch, she fired up and after about three or four minutes, she was "purring like a kitten."

With his hands on his hips, Walter displayed a sense of overall satisfaction with our completion of the repair. We looked back up toward the house on that dark afternoon as electrical lights came on everywhere. It was something to be proud of.

Walking back up to the ranch house, my thoughts were about the title to that song, *Country Folks Will Survive*, and in this case, working together, we had conquered the elements.

After the fourth day and being without electricity two of them, the electricity was reinstated, and Walter flipped the switch on the big generator; it had been a life saver.

They continued to feed the wildlife because the snow was just melting to the point that you could see the ground in places. Most of the wheat stubble was clear of the snow, and upon close observation, quail could be seen venturing out from the brush covered fence rows and into the grain fields.

I remarked to Marjorie that it would be a great time to go quail hunting after the birds had a chance to eat for a day or two without being disturbed. It was near the weekend again, and Marjorie and I decided to go quail hunting Saturday and Sunday morning.

We mentioned to Juanita that we would have plenty of quail for dinner Saturday night if she wanted to prepare them. She was in agreement, and said it was about time for another big meal.

She got no argument out of me or Walter. We were ready.

Saturday morning came, and after a good breakfast, Marjorie and I loaded our gear and the dogs and took off toward the milo fields across the river. It was good and daylight when we put the dogs down just inside the main gate to the big field.

No longer than they ran around and cleaned out did they both lock down in two solid and beautiful points. We stood and admired them as we finished filling our shell bags and loading our shotguns.

Marjorie took the lead toward the point, and I slowly approached from downhill a short distance. She flushed the covey and it was a big one. The majority of them wheeled downhill in my direction.

She dropped three birds on the covey rise, and I emptied my Auto-5 Browning from my excellent position afield. When the smoke cleared, I had seven birds on the ground and the dogs went to work retrieving what we had knocked down.

Marjorie remarked, "Ten birds and you were perfectly positioned to stay on them as they passed in front of you. How did you know that they would turn toward you when they got up?"

"Ninety percent of the time, a flushed covey will follow the terrain unless there are obstructions that steer them on a different flight," was my reply.

"I guess that is one of the tricks of the trade that you learn only with years of field experience," she added.

"Marjorie, today you learned that trick, and I guarantee you that you will never forget it during your future quail hunting days," I told her.

From that day forward, whenever quail hunting with her, I observed her positioning herself for the anticipated direction of flight on the covey rise; she was a quick study and became very proficient with her new trick.

Marjorie and I ended the hunt at noon with our game bags heavy and our shell bags light. It had been another great morning afield and now it was time to return to the ranch house, eat lunch with Juanita and Walter, and clean birds.

Fried quail, cat-head biscuits, and brown gravy was shaping up to be on the evening menu as Marjorie began calling her neighbors to come and dine with us.

About an hour before sundown we had almost 20 guests show up to enjoy dinner with us.

The next morning over breakfast in the kitchen with Marjorie and Juanita, I announced that I would be packing my gear about mid-morning and heading the Suburban back to Northeast Texas. It was almost Christmas and I had to get back home.

It had been a great time spent with friends in the Hill Country and it looked as if I was going to make it home for Christmas. I looked forward to spending the holidays with the family.

The drive in was very relaxing. There was a soft drizzle that hit the windshield the whole trip. It was not hard enough to run the wipers, but an intermittent mode was perfect to keep the glass clean.

Cold rainy days with snow clouds hanging low over the horizons have always held a mysterious attraction for me, and this day was no exception. I drove along and let my mind wander back to hundreds of days spent such as this one, in the field with wonderful friends and great dogs.

While those memories ran free in my mind, the miles passed quickly, and it was not long before I was driving into my driveway.

My son, Trent, was only four years old at the time, and I told him that we would get up early the next morning and go down in Big Cypress Creek Bottom and try our hand at deer hunting. He got all excited, and with his mother's help, started laying out his warm clothes for the trip.

I had a black Chevy Blazer and had the windows darkened for the very purpose of taking him with me and the deer not being able to see him moving around in the truck.

We arrived about an hour before daylight and I located the vehicle in a prime area to see deer moving on a nearby break line. I backed it up into some cover on a fence row and told Trent that we had enough time for about a thirty-minute nap before it would be light enough to see.

I always loved getting to the field early and spending that short time snoozing; it is the best sleeping time in the world.

Many a time I would snooze off thinking that when I awoke there would be a big buck nearby, just waiting on me. On occasion and more than once, he was.

There was an insulated sleeping bag in the back seat, and Trent took advantage of it. It was not long until he was out like a light.

I woke up in about thirty minutes, and it was getting light enough to see about ten yards in front of the Blazer. Another ten minutes and the surroundings were starting to reveal themselves.

I turned around and woke Trent up and told him that he was going to have to help me look for a buck. Instead, he reached into his knapsack and pulled out two cherry-filled long johns.

He sat and ate his with a carton of chocolate milk and watched the windshield for any movement. When he finished the first one, he started on the second but had to quit halfway on it; he was too full to eat anymore. Kids' eyes are always bigger than their stomachs. I think every young person has been told that at least one time growing up.

It was less than ten minutes after it got light enough to see that a nice buck made its way up the draw that led out of the deep bottom and within fifty yards of our vehicle.

After the two of us watched it slowly moving toward us, I rolled the Blazer window down, rested the 270 over the side mirror, and pulled the trigger. It took us about thirty minutes to field dress the eight-point and lay him across the tailgate.

Trent had gotten just enough blood on his camouflage coveralls to show that he had been in the fray. The blood stain was more or less part of a rite of passage for my son. It was his first time to actually be at the scene of a kill; he had partially become a man that morning in Big Cypress Creek Bottom.

The horns still hang on our wall, and Trent still refers to them as "my first buck." It is amazing how far distant an event becomes, sometimes our ownership becomes stronger.

.   .   .

This morning, at the local coffee shop, one of our friends brought a sweet potato pie to have with our morning coffee. That was done from time to time, depending on how generous one of the wives had been with her cooking.

As I partook of my portion, I could not help but think of the best sweet potato pie in the world and how Juanita Sanchez held that title and had held it since I first tasted her pies.

JUANITA'S SWEET POTATO PIE

Juanita managed the kitchen and cooked for Ms. Ada Winslow for 50 years. I was fortunate enough to find both of them in 1979.

There was a spot of ground on Ms. Ada's Oklahoma Panhandle ranch that grew Beauregard Sweet Potatoes that were second to none. The slips were set late, and the potatoes would start coming off about this time of the season.

When the potatoes were dug, washed and cooked, the sugary syrup from them would flow freely, and there was no stringiness to this variety regardless of how big they got.

When I would arrive each year to hunt the ranch, Juanita would be making sweet potato pies almost daily.

I guess the pies and the late November wine made from the sweet potatoes were two of the many things that offered such a strong attraction and kept luring me back up that way for more than thirty years.

They are all gone now but their memories are stored away in the canyons of my mind and will remain there as long as I am alive.

For those dear acquaintances and memories, I would trade nothing.

The satisfaction for me comes now from being able to share those memories through my stories and books.

It is shared for you:

JUANITA'S SWEET POTATO PIE

Ingredients:

$^1/_3$ cup butter
$^1/_2$ cup granulated sugar
2 large eggs slightly beaten
$^3/_4$ cup evaporated milk
2 cups sweet potatoes mashed (bake sweet potatoes in the oven or in the skin in a Dutch Oven with cover to add a unique roasted flavor)
1 teaspoon vanilla
$^1/_2$ teaspoon cinnamon
$^1/_2$ teaspoon nutmeg
Directions:

In mixing bowl:
Cream butter and sugar.
Add eggs mix well.
Add remaining ingredients and mix well.
Add to unbaked pie shell.
Bake in 350-degree oven for 45 minutes to 1 hour or until knife inserted comes out clean.
This makes 1 pie.

.   .   .

After taking Trent deer hunting and processing our deer, it started raining and rained for two weeks. We were fortunate in not having any really cold weather during this time. That saved us from much heartache and also saved our firewood stack.

After several days of steady rain, the bottoms flooded and a couple of us decided to get the big flat bottom out and run out Big Cypress Creek Bottom. That entailed from the east side of Lake Bob Sandlin Dam all the way down to Ferrell's Bridge Dam on beautiful Lake of the Pines.

It was a perfect time to go meat hunting because most of the game could be found on isolated islands in the flooded bottom. Hogs and deer were abundant along with almost all the species of wildlife that inhabited the bottoms.

Through the years, we had harvested many hogs and deer from those spots of high ground, and we knew where they were all located in geographical relationship to the main channel.

One year we killed a mountain lion, and two days later we took a huge male panther that weighed 135 pounds and had been killing livestock in the bottoms for several years; the ranchers were more than happy for our efforts.

Raccoons filled the trees over the water. That was back when their pelts were worth something, and we took enough of them to pay for our efforts.

We killed an abundance of meat, processed it and hauled it into town and gave it to the needy and homebound. It was quite rewarding to all of us to have been involved with this kindness.

BUYING BREEDING STOCK

Marjorie called the first of March and told me that she had spoken with Dr. Lee McKellar in Mt. Pleasant, Texas and had made arrangements with him to come up and look at some registered Brahman heifers and a young bull with Zebu breeding.

Her plans were to be up this way March 15, and she wanted to know if I would meet her and Walter and go with them to the McKellar Ranch. I told her that I would mark it on my calendar and would be ready when they got here.

She also told me that they would be bring their big trailer. Not knowing how many head she would buy, I was asked if I would haul a load back to her ranch if they did make a deal with Dr. McKellar.

As always, I told Marjorie that she could count on me for whatever she needed.

The day arrived for Marjorie and Walter's arrival. I met them for lunch at Pittsburg Hot Links, and we all thoroughly enjoyed the meal. They had both eaten the links before because on more than one occasion I had taken some to the ranch with me when I went down visiting them.

The hot links were very popular with my Hill Country friends; in fact, I have never known anyone that they were not a "hit" with.

I called Oliver McKellar, and he told me that he would meet with us for lunch and then go to the McKellar Ranch with us.

I had known Oliver and Dr. Lee for several years. My dad bought 100 white Brahman heifers from the McKellars back in the late '60s. We were the first family to run Brahman cattle in Camp County.

Everyone was afraid of them and did not want to run them because early on, they did not have the best of a reputation for handling. We learned quickly that the best way to handle the Brahman was with a feed sack or a bucket of range cubes.

It would not take long to gentle a herd down with the cubes; the Brahmans would line up and follow you everywhere in hope of getting another handful thrown their way.

I had Walter and Marjorie both well aware of that technique.

The cross-breeding program that Marjorie was about to engage upon was something that I had encouraged her to do for several years. It was that F1 Brahman Hereford cross that I had fallen in love with through the years of running the cross of cattle and witnessing first-hand what they could do; their offspring seemed to be energized.

After several years of coaxing, I finally got Marjorie to give it a try. That was the reason we were headed to the McKellar Ranch to pick her out some breeding stock.

Dr. Lee had taken off that afternoon and met us at the main pens at ranch headquarters. Per his prior instructions to his ranch hands, there were several pens of cattle that had been rounded up for Marjorie and Walter's visit.

After introductions of everyone present, Marjorie began climbing the fences of the pens and examining the Brahman heifers that weighed approximately 800 pounds each; they were a beautiful bunch of white purebreds.

She was very impressed and turned to me with, "Jim, you were right, they are very impressive animals. I would like to take them all."

She finally climbed off the fences and back on the ground, turning toward Dr. Lee and saying, "Dr. McKellar, sharpen your pencil to a fine point and tell me how much you would take for 100 of these beautiful heifers."

Dr. Lee laughed and replied, "Marjorie, I am going to make you a really good deal on my heifers. They will be taking the McKellar name to the Texas Hill Country."

When he quoted the price, she never blinked.

"I also want a couple of your high-powered young Brahman bulls to breed to some registered Hereford cattle of mine. We are going to cover that F1 cross both ways."

They agreed upon a reasonable price, and Dr. Lee told her that he was going to roll his big trucks and deliver them to her at her ranch between Blanco and Fredericksburg.

Marjorie looked at me and said, "Dr. Lee just did us a big favor and we do not have to worry about hauling them home. If I had known this, we could have left our trailer at the house."

She turned back to Dr. Lee and told him that she would haul the two bulls on her trailer.

Dr. Lee offered to take us up to the Stephens Hotel and buy our dinner. He did not have to offer twice.

Marjorie said she could eat a big steak and feel good about it knowing the size of check that she had just written.

Dr. Lee mentioned over dinner that we were eating choice Angus beef that had been finished on feed in the Texas Panhandle.

"Seldom have I found any that was better," he added.

Marjorie and Walter agreed as we devoured our steaks, baked potato, green salad, rolls and sweet tea.

Marjorie told Dr. Lee she wanted him to visit her ranch in about two years and take a look at what she had done with the infusion of his Brahman blood with her purebred Herefords.

Dr. McKellar promised her that he would do just that. His brother Oliver said that he was going to put it on his calendar to remind him and he was coming with him.

Walter and Marjorie secured rooms for the night at the Gaddis Motel and after a hearty breakfast the next morning they went out to the ranch to follow the cattle trucks back to the Hill Country.

As they pulled out of sight, I thought to myself that the mission I had been on for several years had been completed; a warm wonderful feeling came over me.

Several months later, when visiting Walter and Marjorie during hunting season, I explained the feeling that I had had when they all pulled out of sight, leaving Mount Pleasant, Texas. It was such a feeling as part of me was rolling along with them while leaving some of me behind.

Marjorie loaded me and Walter up in her Suburban and took us to the back pastures where she had the 100 head of white Brahman heifers running with four beautiful Hereford bulls. The cross-breeding program had started.

From there, we drove about a half-mile to a pasture with 50 registered Hereford females and the Red Brahman bulls she had purchased from the McKellar Ranch in Mt. Pleasant. She had the breeding program going full throttle.

"We will have a pasture full of F1s by late June or early July, Jim. You must return next summer and see them as they start to grow and develop."

I told her that I would not miss it for the world. Sensing her excitement made me more than happy.

The first cross between the two different breeds was the strongest; resulting crosses of the F1s started revealing weaker characteristics of both breeds.

It was always my belief that a breeder needed to stop with the first cross and then go outside with another breed. Bringing in the third breed kept the animals highly desirable.

After the first calves from this new breeding program started hitting the ground, she saw the results immediately.

It was 1965, and we had leased 650 acres of pastureland in Prairie Creek Bottom near the foothills of Couch Mountain.

Dr. McKellar had sold us 100 head of beautiful white Brahman heifers that were purebred. Dad and I were so proud of our new acquisitions; it was not uncommon to check on them two or three times a day.

At least once a day we would haul our stock horses with us and ride through the herd, checking to see if all were doing well. As late fall waned in the distance, we were busy getting hay and feed laid by for the winter.

Two days before Christmas that year, we drove down to the Bosque River bottom and picked out four of the prettiest Hereford bulls we could find. They were tall, and they were long, just the type we wanted to breed to our Brahman heifers.

After purchasing them, we hauled them back to Camp County, Texas and went to graining them every day for two reasons: First, moving livestock east requires more nutrition for them until they can adjust to the new climate, and secondly, we wanted them ready for service by the latter part of January.

When it came time to turn the bulls with the heifers, they were in top shape and were looking as good as any breeding stock that we had seen.

The bulls went straight to task and immediately started breeding the Brahman heifers. If everything went well, we would have our F1s hitting the ground in October and November.

Dad and I liked to see our calves born in the fall of the year. That way they were strong enough to make it through our mild winters, and when the grass began greening up in the spring they would be old enough to start grazing on it.

Most years we had winter wheat planted and that allowed the heifers to give plenty of nutritious milk to their babies. This particular year we had planted 150 acres of wheat, and when we turned them on it in January, it was lush green and was about 12 inches tall; it was almost to the point of starting to lodge.

The first-year calf crop was 100%, and we only had to pull two calves that were turned wrong.

After the calves got a little size on them and the mother's milk really kicked in, it was easy to recognize the quality of breeding. It was not uncommon to just stand, watch, and admire what we had; I do not think any two people could have been happier with what they had.

Three years passed, and we had 200 head of the finest F1 Brahman Hereford cattle that most had ever seen.

Dad and I loaded up in July and went to Ohio in search of some Shorthorn bulls to add to our breeding program. We had made several calls to breeders, and everyone kept directing us to the same ranch. We found some fine ones, and after being very selective, we secured ten of them to bring back for our F1s.

We brought them in, penned them together and started our special conditioning program to have them ready to turn out with the females in late December.

For two more years, we kept breeding the Hereford bulls to the Brahman cows, and after that we sold the big Herefords to another breeder. They had infused the amount of Hereford blood that we wanted in our cattle.

The breeder that bought them, after seeing what they produced, paid top dollar for them and was more than happy to get them at that price.

The proceeds from 150 head of F1 cattle started me on my college career and kept me in school during the week. Weekends, I came home to help my dad look after the cattle and land. There was always work to be done, cattle to be taken care of, fences repaired or new fence built.

You can never have enough of pastures and pens when there is such a selective breeding program going on.

We castrated calves as soon as we could after they were born; doing it early hardly affected them.

At six months, we weaned the calves and selected the ones we would turn back for breeders, and the rest were finished on grass in preparation for the market. From there, many of them went on to feedlots to finish them out before slaughter.

We usually butchered two grain fed beeves each year, and the meat was superb; we knew exactly what we were eating.

The Shorthorn bulls on the F1 Brahman Hereford cattle produced some really large-boned cattle. They came along just as what the cattlemen wanted was gradually making a change after the long years of short and fat individuals.

Our offspring exhibited tall, strong qualities of individuals that could carry their weight over wide-open ranges and survive through it. We were convinced after two years that we had the perfect cross for beef production. We had very little pink-eye in our herds because the biggest percentage of our stock carried splotches of dark pigment around their eyes. That characteristic had come from the Brahman Hereford F1 cross.

This is the experience I had with a beef cattle breeding program. This is the experience that I shared with many other cattlemen. This is the experience that I shared with Marjorie Bowles of the Texas Hill Country.

It took about four years to convince her of how she could improve her beef herd of cattle before she really started asking questions.

I guess the turning point was the afternoon that we drove up to Lampasas and visited a fellow rancher that had been friends with me a long time. I had met him several years ago at the Heart of Texas Exposition in Waco where steers from his ranch were consistent winners in the show ring.

He raised the kind of cattle that I had been telling Marjorie about. Like the goats she fell in love with years ago and had to have, she fell in love with these magnificent cattle and had to have some.

"Jim, I guess seeing is believing. How can I get some of those beautiful animals?" she asked me on the way back to her ranch.

I began again to tell her how the F1 cross worked and what we would need to do in order to obtain breeding stock.

"I am ready, and in the meantime, I am going to start culling my commercial herd of cows in preparation for the new breeding," she decided.

"Marjorie, you will not have to be in a hurry to do that because it will take two to three years to start getting your replacements ready to go to work for you."

That brought about the McKellar Connection, the trip to Mt. Pleasant, the meeting with Dr. Lee and Oliver McKellar in hopes of acquiring some of their registered stock; in time, it all came together.

After that acquisition, Marjorie would call at least once a week to keep me posted on the progress of her breeding program. She chuckled loudly when she told me that, "Walter is even excited about what we are doing down here, and he rarely gets excited over anything except hot biscuits, gravy and ribbon cane syrup."

Knowing Walter's penchant for biscuits, gravy and ribbon cane syrup spoke highly of his approval of this latest project that Marjorie had embarked upon.

Her excitement sparked my excitement and I knew the exact feelings that she was having, waiting with great anticipation to see the outcome of her efforts. She was waiting on something that would be hers and hers alone, something to leave to eternity.

We had discussed all of this and like some of our discussions before, tears came to our eyes as we spoke of the future and days that we both yearned to witness.

In fact, we had sat on the benches, overlooking the wildflowers and the River and discussed it all numerous times; our hearts were in sync.

Not many years after I met Marjorie and started spending time with her, Walter, and Juanita, did I come to realize that our associations were meant to be. God had put them in my path, and I was totally blessed to have become part of their lives.

A day with them never passed that I did not think about all of the above, and more than once I thanked God for the loved ones that He had strategically placed in my journey through this world.

TURKEY SEASON ONE MORE TIME

Tomorrow will be April 1, and turkey season will be upon us again. I will pack my gear and return to Marjorie's ranch on the banks of the Pedernales River for some extreme wit-matching with the Rio Grande gobblers.

Walter and I will strip the running gear when we dress them, and Juanita will use them to make dressing. The breasts, like in the past, will be deep-fried in cottonseed oil until they are golden brown.

Marjorie will invite the neighbors, and her violin playing rancher friend from the San Antonio circuit will entertain us with the most beautiful fiddle music you can imagine. I can close my eyes and almost hear the beautiful sounds from her fiddle, floating across the veranda.

Juanita would prepare her holiday dressing with all the trimmings, and we would not hesitate to overindulge.

We held our libations high and toasted Marjorie, and, before the night was over, everything else we could think of. She did so love those occasions for entertaining her friends and having us all together again.

Marjorie would always chuckle when I referred to these specific gatherings as "Thanksgiving in April in the Texas Hill Country."

The parties would last into the night, and there is no past event that stands out in my mind as clearly as under the Texas skies around an open fire-pit, on a crisp April evening, in one of the most beautiful and breathtaking venues in the world.

Those wonderful thoughts down through the years have been a sleep aid for me. Many a night I have drifted off to sleep just thinking about what it was like being there; the impressions were indelible, and the peacefulness was overwhelming.

On at least six different years, I was there for opening turkey season in the spring. I remember so well how witty and wily the turkeys were and how colorful their beautiful plumage was when the morning or evening reflections from the sun hit them just right. I know of no artist that could have mixed the colors on their palette and have come close to doing the reflections justice.

On several occasions, when dressing the gobblers, Walter would skin them and hang the colorful plumage to dry. It was amazing to stand and look at them mounted on a wall under a lean-to on the back side of the barn. Amazingly, you could take a step in either direction and the colorful plumage would change.

I was back down at Marjorie's the first week of June. I had loaded Buck and had taken him with me. Walter called and said there was cowboy work to be done and asked if I wanted to pitch in. I never balked at an opportunity to ride Buck and work cattle, and "cowboy" for a few days.

The first F1 calf crop was going strong and most of them weighed between 400 and 500 pounds. Walter wanted to work the herds, vaccinate the calves, castrate, brand and tag the heifers, and worm all of them.

Once we rounded everything up and got them in the big pens, we started cutting the ones out according to what we were going to do to them.

Marjorie did have some fabulous working pens, and it was no problem separating and penning the ones that needed it. Every run had a squeeze chute on it, and this came in extremely handy for the kind of work we were doing.

Elastrator bands were used on the bull calves to castrate them, and while I was working on one end there was a vaquero on the shoulder area injecting the vaccine and another paste worming. We had quite an assembly line going on our chute, and there were three more chutes with other crews attending them.

In a day's run like we had going, we would turn out many a head that was ready for summer pasture and a small amount of supplement.

Without any unforeseen circumstances, we could turn out approximately 60 calves per hour. Five hundred head a day was our goal when we started, and we knew that we could accomplish that mark.

After we worked all of the F1 calves from the Hereford cattle and Brahman bulls, we turned to the purebreds.

They got the same treatment except for the castrating. Those males passed through the chutes without the elastrator being applied on them. Marjorie sold registered Hereford bulls and would further cull that bunch of calves at a later date.

The Brahman heifers that she purchased and bred to Hereford bulls would start having calves in October, and by the next early summer, those calves would receive the same treatment.

Marjorie would come to the pens at different intervals with cold water and lemonade for all of us. Juanita had made a picnic basket full of pimento cheese sandwiches and cheesecake tea cakes for our lunches, and we would break just long enough to partake of them, get a drink, and return to the working chutes.

Walter and the vaqueros kept the chutes full for us, and there was very little slack time involved with the process.

Marjorie really enjoyed standing and watching us work her herds. Occasionally, she would point a finger and holler out, "There is the kind I am looking for boys."

None of us would even pause when she said it because we had heard it often in the past.

She was so proud of the F1 crosses and could not help but brag on them as they moved through the chutes.

"Jim, I do love them so. Thank you and thank Dr. Lee McKellar for putting me in the business."

The F1s were just remarkable, and there was no doubt of the effect of the infusion of hybrid blood by crossing them up. They were tall, straight, long, and just had that extra look to them; they were a cattleman's dream come true.

After a hard day of working the chutes, Juanita would have superb meals waiting on us each evening. We would come in, take a shower, put on our clean clothes and make it to her table just in time for the serving.

After a fine dinner, generous libations awaited us, and after a few toasts to the heavens, we found our way to bed, knowing that daylight would bring more of the same.

Hard, honest work does wonders for the soul and the perspiration cleans out your system so that you can think clearer. There was always a bunch of clear thinking at Marjorie's during roundup time.

Gosh, I loved it, and now I would trade anything to be able to go back to the ranch and do it one more time after all these years.

After the third day of working the calves, it was time for sorting and deciding which ones would be kept for replacement heifers and which ones would go to the market at Fredericksburg.

The ones selected for replacement heifers were loaded and moved to another part of the ranch where winter pastures were. The heifers that were kept and placed on the green pastures began the second phase of their development.

Quality hay was kept in the hay rings for them to control the amount of scouring that would be brought on by the abundance of green grass. Salt and mineral feeders were also filled to help alleviate any problems along these lines. A ranch vaquero was assigned to ride the herd at least twice a day and check for any signs of bloating.

The male calves were gathered with the heifers that were going to the sale and placed on other winter pastures for 60 days to pick up the weight gain and allow them to bring top dollar at the auction.

At the end of 60 days, most elastrator bands will have cleaned up their work and every calf would be ready for market.

After five days, I loaded Buck and a 550-pound F1 steer that Marjorie gave me to take home and put on feed for the freezer. Periodically, she had done that down through the years. I had learned several years ago not to tell her "no" when she offered me a calf; she kept us in prime beef for years.

I bid everyone farewell and told them that I would be back in September to shoot some dove with them.

Marjorie said, "Jim, make plans to stay a few days when you return, and we will go down to Bandera and look at some Shorthorn bulls."

As I cranked the diesel engine, I replied back to her, "Sounds like a plan to me, my dear. I will see all of you then."

RETURNING HOME

By the time, I got back to Pittsburg, it was almost dark. I unloaded Buck, fed, and stalled him and left the calf on the front of the trailer. Early the next morning would be soon enough to put him in the feed pen that I used specifically to fatten calves for slaughter.

Pilgrim's had a special feed they called Carter's Mix and I started the calf on it along with a couple of blocks of high protein Coastal Bermuda hay twice a day.

Before I penned him, several photos were made so that we might compare future growth after being on feed.

I marked my office calendar as a reminder to pull him off in 120 days and take him to be processed. That would be toward the end of October, and we would have a freezer full of quality meat for the holidays. Thank you, Marjorie Bowles, for your thoughtfulness.

I grained Buck and gave him a couple of blocks of the same high-quality hay. He showed signs of being sore for two or three days after we returned from the Hill Country. It had been several months since he had been called on to work the way he worked for Marjorie. There was some cutting involved and that will show up, especially in a cow horse that had not been worked in a while.

That night, I got a call from Sponge Eubander and his wife, Linda. They wanted me to bring Cortez back up into the Kiamichi Mountains and help them track a killer of calves.

Linda and Sponge had tracked the killer to a conglomerate of caves in the side of a mountain almost to The Winding Stair Mountains. The caves were connected, and there were several outlets that they knew about and told me they were sure that they had not found all the entries and exits.

They went on to say that, "Cortez strikes a 'hot' trail until he gets to the caves and then the trail cools off. The cat is losing him in the caves."

They felt as if the second tracking dog, my Cortez, and my three Ridgebacks would be able to press the cat until it holed up in one location. Once the cat did that, the dogs could find and handle it.

They also told me that the caves were high in the side of a mountain and they used their mules to traverse the terrain. Sponge said we would have to pack in, and it would take at least two to three days to accomplish our mission if we did not run into any unforeseen problems.

Linda mentioned that the caves reminded her of the underground catacomb burial tombs that she had read about that were built by the Romans in days of old. That thought kept returning to me; possibly curiosity, I guessed.

Their call came in on a Wednesday night, and I told them that I would load Thursday morning before daybreak and head their way. Linda volunteered to pack our meals, and I knew what that meant. She would have an assortment of great food and plenty of it.

Anita had prepared a wonderful meal for me and the kids, and we sat and had dinner together and talked about tracking and catching another mountain lion. In the past, I had brought several pictures in for them to see the critters that Cortez and I took out of those hills. After twenty years, it was quite an array.

There were pictures of several big cats and a couple of black bears that we had tracked back to their den and captured them. There were two panthers that came from the flat lands between the mountains; the panthers preferred hanging around closer to a water source.

The mountain lion would range a great distance for water and was not limited to just one locale. This characteristic makes them more vulnerable, at times.

Four-thirty comes early in the morning, and by the time the clock had struck, I was already to the stable and had Rou saddled and loaded on the trailer. Cortez and the three Ridgebacks occupied their usual dog house that was in the front compartment of the gooseneck.

Trixie pounced upon the front seat of the truck; that was her usual place to ride. She could sit up and peer out the windshield. She seemed to sense when we headed north toward the mountains. There was dog food and water on board to last about a week. I had also packed water, hay and grain for Rou.

The mounted water tank over the gooseneck always ensured that we would not run short of water in our travels.

It was not hard to sense the excitement of the dogs. They easily remembered the many times we pulled out before daylight, turning north, and headed to the mountains of Oklahoma.

Rou was a different story. Rou did not get excited until the dogs struck a scent, bayed and found the trail of the critter we were after. As I pulled away from the house, I thought about, "What a team the seven of us make." They had all proven their keep many times over.

I realized that sometimes it takes a lifetime to put together a set of dogs that you are 100 percent confident in and usually know exactly what they will do before they do it. There is so much instinct bred into them.

I crossed Big Cypress Creek Bridge on Highway 271 and was headed north as the sky started showing signs of graying back in the east. That meant that it was about forty minutes before the sun would be peeping at us. Maybe we would be headed north on Highway 259 by then and not have to deal with the early sun in my eyes.

As the sun showed itself, I was crossing The Big Red and noticed that it was really rolling; there must have been quite a bit of rain upstream.

I rolled through Idabel shortly after and continued north on 259 It seemed as if it was getting colder as I traveled up the road. I knew I was gaining elevation; maybe that was why it was feeling cooler.

The sun was up and brightened all the surroundings as I stopped at a red light in Broken Bow. It was the same traffic signal that caught me nearly every time that I passed through. That thought entered my mind, also, as I neared the location of that particular intersection.

It would take near two or more hours to get to Sponge and Linda's ranch that was located almost to Big Cedar. I adjusted the radio and found some mountain music to comfort me in my travels. I thought about what a great feeling to be "as free as the wind," just a man and his dogs, headed on a mission.

It was almost 10:30 in the morning when I pulled across the cattle guard that led onto their ranch and on to their mountain home. As I got closer to the house, I was thinking about all the pleasant times I had had with these two dear friends. I was also thinking about how good Linda looked in her faded jeans and rough out boots.

Faded blue blouse with a light blue leather vest, a short brimmed white Stetson, pulled down on both ends, that covered up her frosted shag haircut;

she had always been a beauty and time had only improved it.

It was about six years ago that she and Sponge accompanied me and Cortez along with my Ridgebacks on another mountain lion hunt and had witnessed firsthand the work of real hunting dogs.

After the hunt, Linda looked at me and asked, "Jim, where can I get me a Cortez and a couple of those Ridgebacks?"

That set my mind in motion that afternoon, and the next morning I replied, "Linda, maybe we can breed you one if I can get in contact with a man in Waskom, Texas that owns a direct son of the original Cortez."

"When will you know?"

From here, this hunt will have to wait until I can catch you up on how Linda and Sponge got their Cortez.

.   .   .

Later that afternoon, Linda asked if I thought she could get puppies similar to Cortez if she bred her best female to a pit bull. I explained how no one could determine how the genetics would play out in the offspring. She understood all of that and reiterated that she was just curious about the possibility of her having a real kill dog, like Cortez.

I mentioned to her that I knew where there was one heck of a pit bull, not too far from where I lived. She asked if I had seen this dog, and I told her that I had only heard of him and had seen a picture of him.

"He really favors my Cortez," I added.

"Jim, do you think you can get my Ellie bred to him?" was her next question.

"As soon as I can find the numbers and make a couple of phone calls. I should know something within two to three days."

I told her I would make the calls and see if that was possible. I told her to remind me after dinner, and I would call Nita at home and have her retrieve the telephone numbers. Then I would make the calls to see if I could set it up for her.

Sponge was listening to our conversation, but he had not commented one way or the other. He knew how important things could become with Linda once she made her mind up.

Later that evening, after a wonderful meal in her beautiful kitchen, Linda handed me the phone. I knew better than to ask her if she was sure she wanted to do this; she had already locked it in her head.

I called Nita and got the numbers, and after three phone calls, I finally got the owner of the dog on the phone and went through a long explanation of who I was and why I was calling.

He told me that it was our responsibility to get the female to him, and he would want her as soon as we could deliver. He wanted her settled and comfortable to the new surroundings before ever thinking about putting her with the male.

He went on to say that when she was bred we would need to come and pick her up. At that time, he would want $750 for the breeding fee.

He explained that he had a very high percentage success rate on the first breeding. I told him to give me a few minutes and let me explain all of this information to the owner of the female.

After I explained everything to Linda, she said she was ready to take Ellie to him.

I called the man back and told him we were ready. He asked me when we would be there with the female. I explained that I lived fairly close to him and would bring the female back to Texas with me when I returned in about a week. I would call him at that time and set a time to meet with him and deliver Ellie.

He was okay with those plans, and when I hung the phone up Linda was jubilant. I told her not to get too excited because we were "rolling the dice" on this breeding in trying to get what she wanted; Sponge agreed.

I explained to her that the odds were against us. Sometimes you can lay out all the right plans and the results turn out just opposite to what you had planned. I went on to explain that I had no idea that my Cortez was going to turn out like he did. I did know that I was lining the stars up the best that I could for it to happen as I had planned.

The exceptional individuals appear from time to time and no one can explain how it happens nor can they predict the frequency of it happening. It just happens.

In 30 years of breeding bird dogs, it has happened for me twice. Looking back now, those are small odds, and had I known those odds going in, I might not have even tried it. Then, on the other hand, I think about those two exceptional individuals and realize that if I had not ever tried it, I would never have had the pleasure of following them afield and watching them perform. I readily admit now that it was all worth it.

Sponge and Linda listened to me ramble on with my own beliefs about breeding practices, and when I finished they both nodded toward me and said that they were glad they were giving it a try also. They were rolling the dice and hoping for a win.

On Sunday morning, I loaded Ellie, hugged Linda and Sponge goodbye, and set out for the Red River, headed home. When I arrived home, I called the man with the pit bull and made arrangements to bring Ellie to him the very next morning.

It was about an hour and a half drive to Waskom to deliver Ellie to the breeder. Following the man's directions closely, I drove straight to his house on the outskirts of town.

He met me in the driveway, and we shook hands. We visited for a while and then he asked if I was ready to see Justice. I told him that I was, and I also told him I had seen his picture a couple of years ago.

We rounded the corner of the kennels, and there he was. I do not believe I have ever seen a finer specimen of Pit Bull flesh. He was tall, he was wide through the chest, he had a large wide head, his girth was deep, and the slope to his back was perfect.

I told his owner that I was very impressed with Justice and asked him to give me some background on the dog. He did, and as he was talking I realized that Justice had the same father as my Cortez. This dog was kin to my Cortez and to the original border fighter, Cortez.

In my mind, the chances of great pups out of Justice and Ellie just increased; I definitely became excited with the cross.

When I arrived back at my house, I called Linda and Sponge and told them what I had observed and what I had been told. My excitement carried over to them as we discussed the increased possibilities of some really great pups.

I told Linda I would pay half of the breeding fee to get a female out of the cross. She said that I would do no such thing and that my pick of the females was my decision; I could have any one of them that I wanted.

All three of us were kids again, and Christmas was coming. I told them I would return with Ellie when the man called me. Linda said they might drive down to meet me when she was ready to come home.

My imagination ran wild as I thought about the possibility of raising a third line descendent of the famous Cortez. She had to be something else.

The Eubanders and I spoke many times while we were waiting on the breeder to give us a call. Linda remarked that she would possibly keep all the males in hopes of having one that was as great as my Cortez.

The second week of March, the breeder called and said that Ellie was ready to come home. I told him that I would be in Waskom the first thing the next morning.

At nine o'clock, I rolled into the breeder's driveway, and he met me when I got out of my truck. We talked for a moment and then we retrieved Ellie from the kennel. I noticed that she had fleshed up some in the absence of exercise.

I paid the breeder the required amount, and we loaded Ellie into the dog box in the back of my Dodge dually.

As we were standing around the truck talking, the subject of my Cortez came up and the breeder wanted to know how he was crossed up. I explained how I had raised a nice Ridgeback Cur female out of a cross between the border fame Cortez and my female Ridgeback Cur.

He asked me about the owner of Cortez, and I told him it was a lady I had befriended several years ago. I explained about hauling my female all the way to Three Rivers to get her bred.

The breeder looked me in the eye and asked me how well I knew the lady that owned Cortez. I told him I did not know her socially, but I had had a couple of dealings with her in the San Antonio area.

He went on to explain that she got Cortez from her father. Her father fought dogs all up and down both sides of the border for years, before he passed away. Supposedly, he was more well-known than the dogs in his string. He had raised Cortez from a pup and had trained him to fight.

It was rumored around in the dog fighting circles that Cortez had won well over $300,000 in the pit. He fought five years and retired undefeated. The lady's father had turned down $70,000 for him, shortly before he passed away.

All of this was news to me, but I thanked the breeder for sharing the information with me. Originally, I had only bits and pieces of the story. The breeder went on to tell me that the last fight Cortez had was with a huge dog from Matamoros.

The two owners agreed to fight the two dogs for ownership or what was left after the fight.

Cortez won the fight and was injured during the battle. He sustained a deep cut to his left shoulder but went on to kill the other dog. That was his last fight, and he retired a champion.

The breeder went on to ask me more questions about my Cortez. I had pictures on the dash and showed him my dog. He asked if I would sell him and I answered, "definitely not."

He asked me what I used Cortez for, and I told him that Cortez was used for several things. He was a cow dog, a hog-dog, a panther and cougar killer, and a dedicated pal. He was my heavy lifter, but he was gentle enough to babysit the kids in the back yard.

I shook the man's hand and got into my truck. I drove back to Daingerfield and hit 259 North on my way to the foothills of The Winding Stair Mountains. On the way, I called Linda and told her that I was headed to their ranch. In the background, I heard Sponge celebrating; we were all excited about this litter.

I dropped Ellie off and ate a late lunch with Sponge and Linda before I turned back south. It had been a full day, and I was ready to get home.

They bid me farewell and I left out.

The second week of May, Linda called and said Ellie had six males and five females. Mom and all the puppies were doing great. I told her how excited I was for them and for her to keep me posted on the progress of the pups.

We stayed in touch about twice a week until I loaded up and headed north; that was the middle of July. The pups were about eight weeks old, and I could not believe how big they were. They were beautiful and not nearly as awkward as I remember Pit Bull puppies being.

I played with them all the next morning before finally deciding on the female I wanted. I picked out the female that was lightest in color. I wanted my hog dogs light in color in case they were injured fighting a hog and were bleeding; I wanted to see the blood immediately.

Many of their injuries could be tended in the field if they were discovered soon enough. Several nights we have had to sew our dogs up from gashes and deep cuts from the tusks of the wild hogs.

After I made it known which female I wanted, Linda remarked to Sponge that I had chosen the one that she said I would choose. I looked at her, smiled, and said, "Linda, great minds think alike."

She cooked us a wonderful dinner that evening, and we sat down to a fine meal that was prepared by a superb cook. She had chicken fried steak, mashed potatoes, fried fresh corn from the cob, broiled asparagus from her beds, homemade-from-scratch rolls and sweet iced tea. For dessert, she served us her triple layer coconut cake.

Words could not describe how good the meal was and words could never reflect the depth of our friendship; the hill people are kind of special, in their own way.

LINDA'S CHICKEN FRIED STEAK AND GRAVY

Ingredients:

4 ($^{1}/_{2}$ pound) beef cube steaks
2 cups all-purpose flour
2 tsp. baking powder
1 tsp. baking soda
1 tsp. black pepper
$^{3}/_{4}$ tsp. salt
1$^{1}/_{2}$ cups buttermilk
1 egg
1 Tbsp. hot pepper sauce (e.g. Tabasco™)
2 cloves garlic, minced
3 cups vegetable shortening for deep frying

$^{1}/_{4}$ cup all-purpose flour
4 cups milk
Kosher salt and ground black pepper to taste

Directions:

Pound the steaks to about $^{1}/_{4}$-inch thickness.

Place 2 cups of flour in a shallow bowl. Stir together the baking powder, baking soda, pepper and salt in a separate shallow bowl; stir in the buttermilk, egg Tabasco sauce, and garlic.

Dredge each steak first in the flour, then in the batter, and again in the flour. Pat the flour onto the surface of each steak so they are completely coated with dry flour.

Heat the shortening in a deep cast-iron skillet to 325 degrees. Fry the steaks until evenly golden brown, 3 to 5 minutes per side.

Place fried steaks on a plate with paper towels to drain. Drain the fat from the skillet, reserving $^{1}/_{4}$ cup of the liquid and as much of the solid remnants as possible.

Return the skillet to medium-low heat with the reserved oil. Whisk the remaining flour into the oil. Scrape the bottom of the pan with a spatula to release solids into the gravy. Stir in the milk, raise the heat to medium, and bring the gravy to a simmer. Cook until thick, 6 to 7 minutes. Season with kosher salt and pepper.

Spoon the gravy over the steaks to serve.

LINDA'S MASHED POTATOES

Ingredients:

1-pound baking potatoes, peeled and quartered
2 tablespoons butter
1 cup milk
Salt and pepper to taste

Directions:

Bring a pot of salted water to a boil. Add potatoes and cook until tender but still firm, about 15 minutes; drain.

In a small saucepan heat butter and milk over low heat until butter is melted.

Using a potato masher or electric beater, slowly blend milk mixture into potatoes until smooth and creamy.

LINDA'S TRIPLE LAYER COCONUT CAKE

Ingredients:

Cake:
$1/2$ cup salted butter softened
$1/2$ cup vegetable oil
1½ cups sugar
2 teaspoons coconut extract
6 large egg whites room temperature
$1^1/_2$ cups coconut milk
$1/4$ cup sour cream
3½ cups cake flour
4 teaspoons of baking powder
½ teaspoon salt

Frosting:
16 ounces of cream cheese softened
1 cup salted butter softened
1 teaspoon coconut extract
3 cups powdered sugar
3 cups coconut flakes

Instructions:

Grease three 9-inch pans. Line the bottom with parchment paper. Preheat an oven to 350 degrees F.

In a large mixing bowl, use a hand mixer to cream

the butter, oil, and sugar together until smooth. Beat in coconut extract and egg whites 2 minutes until fluffy. Beat in coconut milk and sour cream until just combined.

Mix in cake flour, baking powder, and salt until just combined.

Divide the batter among the three prepared pans. Bake at 350 for 25 to 30 minutes. Let sit in pans for 5 minutes and then transfer to a wire rack to cool completely before layering and frosting.

Make the frosting by using a hand mixer to beat cream cheese and butter together for 1 minute until light and fluffy. Add in coconut extract and mix until combined, about 10 seconds.

Slowly add in powdered sugar, one half cup at a time until smooth, mixing between additions.

Frost and layer cake with frosting and use coconut flakes to coat.

After the fine meal, we retired to the big room and Linda asked me to tell the story that she loved dearly, the one about the hunting friend in the mountains that had passed away and I would return and visit him from time to time.

Nothing delighted me more.

RETURNING A FAVOR

Why does the chill of cold wintry rainy afternoons have such an effect on me? I have thought about it often and at length, but the answer has yet to be found.

It could be the relationship to many successful days afield that bring the special feelings back to me. It could be the many hunting and fishing acquaintances that share the near feelings. Or, it might just be the memories of those friends and days past that keep coming back to me with the onset of cold wintry rainy afternoons. Whatever the reasons, the feelings are always most welcomed.

As I sit and ponder the question again, my mind drifts back to an afternoon high in the Kiamichi Mountains when I stopped by a family cemetery to check on an old friend and sit with him awhile. I knew that he would appreciate the visit and that his family would not mind me stopping by to say "hello."

While he was living, he reminded me on different occasions that I owed him several favors during our friendship and one of the favors he wanted returned was when we got old for me to drop by and visit with him from time to time. In return, he would come and visit me. Today, like several days in the past, I was returning a favor.

As I sat on the large mountain stone, that served as his headstone, I remembered the cold wintry rainy afternoon that we laid him to rest. It was an afternoon like so many the two of us had spent hunting the clear-cuts, high in the mountains.

The preacher gave a short eulogy and several of his other friends joined in. I chose to remain silent and could not have spoken if I had tried. I just sat there, misty eyed, and thought about all the good times we shared.

On this visitation, it had been almost seven years since we had his service. I felt the cold wind on the back of my neck and thought how my friend often remarked on such an afternoon that God was guiding us down the mountain and back to the truck.

Looking back, that expression did not really sink in. After his death and with each passing year it becomes more evident to me exactly what my friend meant.

Our hunts were numerous and during hunting season we went every day that we could. Most of the time I would headquarter in Broken Bow and drive up into the mountains to hunt. Other times we would stay in his cabin, high in the mountains.

He had an old civil war cannon he had refurbished and mounted and every New Year's Eve he would fire it in celebration. I was there for the tradition several times but now as I look back...I wish I could have been there more.

Early one morning I pulled up in front of his cabin. It was a couple of hours before daybreak and he already had a fire going and coffee on. We drank coffee as he cooked breakfast for us.

Cured mountain ham, fried potatoes, scrambled eggs, white peppered skillet gravy, wild muscadine jelly and "cathead" biscuits. It was a cold morning and the hearty breakfast fit right in.

The hunts are still vivid in my memory. The dogs would run out in front of us, into the wind, and stop occasionally, their heads held high, to sniff the elusive mountain quail.

Hunting rough terrain could be dangerous at times, especially over new ground that we had not previously hunted. The comfort was in returning to the safety of the truck after a long hunt.

Some days our hunts would be so extensive that we would need a compass to find our way back to where we had started. It was not unusual for us to cover 10 to 12 miles and over rough ground that is a very intensive hunt.

Over the years, we hunted an area that ranged from Ludlow to Neshoba. Northern McCurtain County, Pushmataha, and Southern LeFlore were our stomping grounds. We hunted from Cloudy to Three Sticks with Battiest, Bethel, Clebit and Pickens, a stop for lunch.

What Weyerhaueser did not own, we had permission from other landowners to hunt. After a long day of quail hunting, it was always such a comfort to top that last rise and see familiar surroundings that marked our way back to the truck.

Sitting on the mountain stone and rubbing the bronze plaque carried me back to those days and the thought and experiences associated with them.

While together, we would often talk about how unexpected the mountain showers could come and go. How we could see the rain coming long before we could hear it... re-emphasizing the vastness of the locale.

Sitting there and looking back down the side of the mountain, noticing how the surroundings had taken on such a wintry appearance, called to mind a late season hunt we had, not too far from here.

That day was a lot like this one, only that it had

started out good and as it progressed it worsened. By mid-afternoon we were miles from the truck and began to encounter snow flurries. The temperature was dropping, and the wind was chasing down the hollows. By late afternoon we made it back to the vehicle and loaded the dogs.

On an earlier hunt, I brought my friend a bushel of sweet potatoes from my garden. He had taken the potatoes and made wine out of them.

As we sat together in the warm truck and watched the snow blow off the windows, we partook of our labors. It was a delightful day for such an experience. How fitting were the moments...a dry wine after a cold hunt.

We stopped hunting the clear-cuts years ago and the road hunting that we resorted to after we reached an age where we could not withstand the ruggedness...has long been set aside.

Our dogs are all gone, and their bloodlines have been immersed across the bloodlines of other memorable hunting stock. The life afield behind those papered names can only be reflected by their respective owners, and many of us are gone too.

These are the things that we talked about when we were together. As I look back, the depth of our discussions was very intriguing. Today it offers a lot of grist for me to mill in my mind. For this, I am eternally thankful.

Our conversations entertained us back then and recalling those conversations entertains me today. It is all about the memories, and together we made many of them. It all came to me in a dream recently and I decided only a few days ago to share these thoughts in my writing. My friend would have liked that very much. He loved reminiscing.

He was ten years older, and we had met one night at the country club in Idabel. Weyerhaueser was hosting a big reception and another friend of mine introduced us.

That was in 1972, and we went on our first bird hunt the following weekend. After that, we were almost inseparable during hunting season. He was the one that introduced me to the Kiamichis. For that, I am also very thankful.

He was a simple man with very little formal education, but he was wise in so many different ways. His kind was referred to by the "locals" as the "mountain boys."

He ranged cattle and hogs across the open lands that were owned and managed by the large timber company. He would roundup the stock twice a year and the roundups would take two or three days. Such a roundup was quite a test for a good horse.

On three different occasions, I hauled my horse north and made the mountain roundup with him and some of his companions. Those companions served as pallbearers at his funeral.

Simple men have simple ways, and my friend was no exception. He put very little stock in the glitter and frill of objects. His litmus was for the usefulness of an item; it either passed the test or not...there were no in-betweens.

His silver was found in the cloud linings of a clearing sky, and his gold was concealed in the heavy-laden bird covers of autumn. He had what he needed and wanted for nothing more.

I bought him a new pair of Tony Lamas for Christmas one year, and when I gave them to him he folded them up and submerged them in a horse trough.

Surprisingly, I looked at his wife and she remarked, "We can't buy him anything new."

Later he explained to me how he broke the new leather in by first putting it in the horse trough and later by drying and conditioning it with bear grease and turpentine.

Saddles, bridles, boots, scabbards, belts, and all other items of leather went through the same process. Many of his articles had lasted a lifetime, and looking back now, I guess that was a pretty good litmus.

Late fall would bring the coronation to the mountains in the form of the blood red blackjacks on the sides of the hills. One could stand on a high vantage point and count almost each and every one of the them.

Such a vantage point was on a bend overlooking the Eagle Fork River that we used as a turkey camp for several years. We stood there many times, at different intervals of the day, and took inventory of God's handiwork.

The afternoon was getting late and the wind kept whipping over my duster and off the back of my hat as if to remind me once again that it was time to move on down the mountain.

As in times past, I was hesitant to leave my old friend. After a while, I arose from his headstone, turned the collar of my duster up, pulled my hat down and bid him farewell again...not knowing when or if I would return.

But I will head north again this year, after the summer heat breaks and the weather turns colder. I will be going back to ride in the mountains and to sit and visit with him.

It could possibly be on a cold wintry rainy afternoon when I return. I know that we both would like that very much.

When I finished, Linda was all teary eyed and made the remark that she cried over very few things. She cried at funerals, at weddings, and when I told one of my stories. I hugged her tight and told her that it was perfectly all right for her to cry when listening to my story. I admitted to her that sometimes I cry just thinking about the occasions described.

SELECTING THAT SPECIAL PUPPY

By the end of the summer, Linda had just about decided on the one male puppy that was going to be her Cortez. All during the summer, she had put them all through a battery of tests daily, trying to distinguish the one pup she was looking for. She had a red collar, and she used it to mark the pup that had scored the highest on her latest test. It was all very amusing to Spongell.

During the last two months, each puppy had an opportunity to don the red color for a period of time. Linda had a way of keeping score on their progress of accomplishing her feats.

Sponge explained to me that all the male pups had the potential of making excellent dogs, but Linda was looking for that special one.

When I returned to their ranch in the middle of October, Linda had made her final decision, and her Cortez had been selected to carry on the tradition.

I was content in knowing that there was a Cortez in the mountains now, and I could imagine how things were going to be different.

I spent quite an amount of time with her selection and after a couple of days, I told her that I thought she made the right decision. That pleased her.

If the need for a dog with special talents presented itself, Linda and Sponge had one. There would be nothing more exciting than to be called on to complete a special mission. Linda and Sponge had served on such a mission with me, and now they were awaiting the time to return to such a circumstance; I was proud of them and for them.

Linda and Sponge had the other five males spoken for and received $1,000 for each pup. The new owners had already selected and picked up their new charges. Most of them went to area locals, but one went all the way to Missouri. There was a middle-age couple in Joplin that had bought a puppy from them before.

Linda kept two of the females and sold the remaining two. A lady from Arkansas bought both of them. During my October visit, the lady from Ft. Smith drove down and picked up her two pups.

We visited at length about their capabilities.

And what about my pup, you might ask. I named her Trixie, and she was growing like a weed. She rode in the front seat with me and accompanied me wherever I went. She slept on the floor next to my bed, and if I got up during the night, she was with me.

I had found another friend, or, she had found me.

I started Trixie in the cattle pens with me as we worked cattle and moved them around and into the chutes and other pens. Trixie was progressing nicely, if I could get her to stay out from under my feet.

Every time I turned around, she was tripping me with her closeness. She developed that in the cattle working pens with me when, as a pup, she stayed away from the cattle, and especially the ones with the long horns.

Trixie started running the hog traps with me after she got a little older and started getting the smell of the wild hogs in her mind. She would hop off the Kubota and charge the traps when they held the hogs.

The hogs would go wild, and Trixie would bark at them as she worked around them as if she was herding them. It was a sight to behold.

We were waiting on cooler weather now and we would start running the hogs at night with the big dogs. And yes, her dad, old Cortez, would probably lead the pack.

And that catches you, the reader, up on how it all came about and how Linda and Sponge got their Cortez.

And back to the story: Sponge and Linda met me in the driveway and after our greetings, we sat at their breakfast table and had a cup of dripped Folgers coffee and soft tea cakes sprinkled with coconut; what a treat.

As we partook of our refreshments, they began telling me of the incidents that had led up to this morning.

Two weeks ago, they lost a calf that was about a week old. After searching with their Cortez and the Curs, they finally found the body of the calf about 100 yards from where it was killed. When the dogs located the body covered with grass, they remembered how we had determined in the past that it was signs of a cat.

A mountain lion will make the initial kill, drag the prey a short distance, cover it with grass or other natural material, and return to it within the next few days to drag it to its den.

About three days later, the calf's body disappeared and their Cortez and the Curs had followed the dragged trail about three miles as it kept ascending into the mountains.

Finally, they came to a conglomeration of caves high and on the north side of a mountain. This is where the trail ended, and the dogs were called off because of the dangers of fighting the cat in close quarters. It is to a cat's advantage to get a pursuer in close quarters so that they cannot move, and the cat can kill them.

These caves were not very large in circumference; they were probably only three to four feet in the largest places. A man could have crawled through the caverns had he been brave enough to do so. A dog could have easily passed through them if it had not been for the dangers of being attacked in close quarters.

The next morning, Linda and Sponge went back to the cave with Cortez, but he was handicapped when they discovered there were several entrances and exits to the caves. Scent was everywhere but it could not be distinguished in one certain area; at that point, they both decided that they needed help in trapping the critter before it could crawl out another hole and escape.

That is when they called me for my help and prompted this story.

Trixie was sitting in the front seat of the dually and acting like the privileged dog that she was, when I drove up and Linda reached in to pet her on the head. That is all it took for Trixie to start whining, slobbering, and wanting to go to her.

It only got worse when Linda opened the truck door and let her out. Trixie, forgetting that she was no longer just a puppy, immediately wanted Linda to pick her up.

As we all walked toward the house, Trixie finally gave up on that idea.

As we were sitting, eating tea cakes, and drinking our coffee, Sponge and Linda told me that they had lost another calf and the cat must be working closer to the ranch house because two of their pygmy goats had gone missing two nights ago. They went on to explain that they never lose a goat; they are there for their twice a day feeding.

I explained that something was wrong because a mountain lion would only kill one goat at a time. There must be more than one cat involved. They said that they had taken the dogs and had searched for the pygmy goats to no avail.

I explained that since the goats were smaller than a baby calf, the lion or lions must have taken them farther up into the mountains before hiding them out and covering them with debris. I went on to say that I was surprised that their dogs could not cut a scent on the drag trail.

"But they could," answered Sponge, "They just could not stay with it until they found the goats. Something kept throwing them off."

"When we get to the base of the mountains, let's turn out my dogs and keep your dogs in the boxes until we can determine more about what is going on. I am ready to hit the trail as soon as I can get Rou unloaded and saddled. Get your mules ready and load your dogs in the boxes," was my reply as we all got up from the breakfast table.

In less than thirty minutes, we were all loaded, pulled out of the driveway, and headed north to begin the hunt.

In about fifteen minutes, we pulled of onto a logging road and headed due west. I could sense we were returning to the large valley that was on the left just before 259 reached the foothills of The Winding Stair Mountains. I had been in that valley many times in the previous years.

It was the same valley that prior to the bad spell of weather that was forecasted, we had worked the cattle out of the hills and assembled them in the valley below to feed them and herd them to safe pastures. It was such a monumental job.

Thinking about that mountain trail drive several years ago brought a smile to my face; we all had had a ball for a few days, working together, being a cowboy, and enjoying each other's companionship.

Most of those companions are still living with the exception of Slim Jenkins, the chief cook and fire tender. He was forever loved by all of us.

Then, there was our friend that died from the Agent Orange poisoning that he received while serving America in the Vietnam War. Sadness always returned to us when we discussed losing him from our group.

After two or three more miles, we came to the stopping point and parked our trucks and trailers. I turned Cortez and the Ridgebacks out to give them time to clean out after the ride north.

Trixie had bounced out of the front seat by the time I was saddling Rou. When finished, I tied him to the outside of the trailer to allow me time to get our other gear for the day together.

We had our "slickers," our bedrolls and our saddle bags. When all of those were put in place, all three of us were ready to start the tracking up the mountain.

Sponge and Linda left their dogs in their trailer until we found out more about what we were tracking.

We all hit the trail as I motioned the dogs on out to look for scent. Maybe, if they could pick up the scent, we could read the signs and determine more about our hunt.

We had only traveled about 200 yards when I noticed the pace of Cortez had picked up and at about the same place the Ridgebacks became alerted; we had a scent.

When Sponge, Linda and I reached that particular spot, we cut sign on a good set of cat tracks in the dirt and knew we had made a strike.

The dogs were moving quicker now and to keep them in sight, we had to pick up our pace.

That was no problem for Rou because of his love for action and he had been in on the action numerous times in our hunts of his past.

Riding him, I could sense the change in his behavior; there was more of a bounce in his step.

Linda and Sponge were right with us on their mules, and we were moving at a good clip. The dogs could be seen from a distance, and they were gaining elevation as they moved out in front of us.

According to Sponge, the dogs were headed in the direction of the catacomb caves atop the mountain.

As we ascended the mountain, it was obvious to me that we were in mountain lion country; there was a lack of small animals. We had not seen any opossums, raccoons, armadillos or rabbits. The cats will eat all the smaller animals except for the skunks and the porcupines.

In a few minutes, the sound of the dogs changed, and experience told us that they had bayed. As we moved up the trail, we came upon the dogs; they had found the bodies of the pygmy goats.

The sign on the goats was evident of a kill by a cat. We pulled off of the carcasses and with a whistle and a motion of the hand, the dogs were trailing again.

It was almost an hour and a half more when we finally ascended the heights and arrived at the caves.

Linda and Sponge began pointing out openings in the side of the crest. The dogs moved from one opening to another just sniffing and whimpering in a low partial growl.

Scent was everywhere, and we had arrived where the cat or cats slept.

Cortez and the Ridgebacks acted as if they were going to enter the caves until I made it clear to them that we were not going in after our prey.
We spent several minutes walking around and examining the openings before we broke for lunch.

During lunch, Sponge asked, "How are going to get them out of their den?"

"I have been giving much thought to that, my friend, and I think the only way to do it is with fire," was my reply.

I went on to explain that the cave openings were on the north side of the mountain and there were only three openings that we knew of on the south side. Smoke would drive them from their den.

Let's go back to the house and prepare for in the morning. We will need charcoal, lighter fluid, green pine boughs and patience.

Early the next morning, we returned with everything that we had gone after. Sponge and Linda brought their dogs along this time, and we had quite a bunch of them - seven all together.

Upon arrival at the caves, we proceeded to the north side of the mountain, and as the three of us on mules and the seven dogs had swept the hillside, we felt pretty sure that any mountain lion that might have been out was back and holding tight in the caves.

Our dogs had hit fresh scent a time or two coming up the slopes and the trails led to the caves.

We poured a small stack of charcoal briquettes on the ground in front of each cave opening on the north slope. We expected the prevailing north wind to carry our heavy smoke down and through the caves.

We cut green pine boughs and after the coals were hot we began placing the pine boughs on top; they did create a heavy dark smoke as it entered the caves. The slight breeze from the north was carrying the smoke just as we had intended for it to do. Our plan was coming together.

I asked Linda and Sponge to take the dogs and position themselves on the south side of the slope and be ready for any evading cat. Linda had drawn her 270 from its scabbard that was made to carry from her saddle. I knew what that meant because her shooting prowess was well known in our group.

The smoke only got heavier as the coals got hotter and the pine needle smoke was rolling off the stacks of charcoal.

It took approximately 25-30 minutes before I heard any action from the south side of the caves. There were two shots and then a delay before a third shot was fired; Linda had her 270 talking and there was no doubt in my mind about her hitting her targets.

I saw her miss a spike buck back several years ago. She was on horseback, the buck was running hard, and it was about 220 yards from us. She kept saying that she thought she hit him. The next day, she shot a spike that turned out to be the same one, and he had a fresh crease over the top of his shoulders. Linda had not missed him; she just did not bring him down.

As I sat in the saddle, bits and pieces of that particular afternoon began coming back to me. It was slow at first, and then it seemed as if everything fell into place and came back to vividly portray the day that was not much different from the one at hand.

As I rode around to the other side of the mountain top, I thought about that afternoon and thought about all those memories that I had forgotten that were triggered by who knows what. They were just precious memories and I was so pleased that they did return as they had.

My dogs were trailling me, and Linda and Sponge had their dogs with them. When I did arrive at their location, they had two mountain lions laid out side by side, and in a distant I could see their Cortez dragging a third one to the group of two.

Linda was wiping down her 270 and returning it to its fleece-lined saddle holster. She looked up at me and said that they had been very successful handling the cats, once they broke from the caverns.

"The smoke did the trick, Jim. They seemed a bit addled the first few minutes out of the caves and away from the heavy smoke," she said.

The smoke had driven them out, and the mountain lions wanted nothing to do with what they thought was an approaching wildfire. I had seen that trick used several years ago in northern New Mexico on a Mescalero Apache reservation, bear hunting.

Another friend, High Eagle of the Apache Nation, commonly known as Harold Waters, had used the smoke to drive the bears from seclusion. I had been there to witness it all and remembered it when thinking about getting the mountain lions to move from the caverns.

After their Cortez reached us, dragging the third mountain lion, we examined all three closely and found that they were all females. We determined that the mother and two of her offspring were living in the caves and were the culprits guilty of killing their livestock.

Sure Foot, our pack mule, had gotten their scent and was none too excited about carrying the cats back down the mountain. After we laid them across the rack and secured them, he settled down. Once the cats were in place, he realized they were dead and were of no danger to him.

After a lengthy conversation, we loaded all of our gear and started the slow trek back down the mountains. It had been a good hunt, and we had been successful while not incurring much difficulty; that was plenty to be thankful for.

Old stories of this and our adventures of the past flowed freely as we made the trip back to the trucks and trailers. Someone just standing and observing our behavior might think that we were a band of mountain gypsies just making our merry way down the hills; the air was filled with laughter and love.

It would have been a perfect time for a master musician to have pulled a bow across a finely tuned violin. That background music would have been perfect to have ended the day and the story.

Back at the trucks, we loaded everyone and laid the cats across the bed of Sponge's dually. When we arrived back at their house, Linda fetched the camera from their ranch house and took pictures of all of us with our prey.

We laughed again and continued to tell stories of our past days afield, hunting and tracking.

Linda went in and told us that she would start supper for us if we would take care of the stock and feed the dogs before putting them in their pens. Sponge and I were in agreement that this was a more than fair trade, and we got busy with our chores.

In about an hour we entered the back door to the smell of chicken fried steak, hot cathead biscuits, and brown skillet gravy. Linda had done it again.

When our meal was finished, she surprised us with her triple layer coconut cake, that she had prepared the afternoon before; she knew how I always carried on about her coconut cake.

After dinner, we sat in the living room, took regular libations of mountain wild strawberry wine, and visited to almost twelve o'clock, before turning in for the night.

As I drifted off to sleep, my thoughts returned to that afternoon trip down the mountains and the imaginary fiddle music flowing through the trees and up and down the draws. What beautiful Kiamichi thoughts to fall asleep to; my beautiful Kiamichi home.

It was almost seven o'clock the next morning when I was awakened by Linda rattling pots and pans in the kitchen. There was also a smell of strong coffee drifting about the house.

Sponge and I took our coffee on the back porch with Linda. After two or three cups each, we arose from the cane-bottomed wooden chairs and made our way to the barn. We had livestock to feed, mules to grain, and sack feed for the dogs.

I fed Ames Dog Food, and when I was on the road it went with us. My dogs expected it and if they were going to work up to my expectations, they were going to get Ames.

I have known friends that had tried to skimp and save on dog food. My experiences that were passed on to me at an early age by sure-enough dog men always demanded that our dogs received the best food we could give them. When they were being worked hard, they would receive a double ration.

I could look at the coat of hair on a dog and how much flesh he was carrying and almost tell you if the dog was being worked adequately and fed right, one-hundred percent of the time.

I guess that is not too much to be able to show after all those years in the field with all the different dogs that I owned, but it was something that I could pass on to my readers or to any others that might have a desire to know about such things.

After all the stock was fed and the dogs taken care of, we worked our way back up to the house to visit with Linda before I had to load my stuff and hit the road back south to Texas.

I had promised Anita that we would take the kids down to Johnson Creek Campground on beautiful Lake of the Pines. My intentions were to get home, hook to the fifth wheel, and head to the lake for several days.

As we walked into the house, I pulled the pictures of the steer calf that Marjorie had given me to feed out for the freezer and showed them to Sponge and Linda.

Immediately, Linda said, "We must have some of these calves, Jim.

What are they and where did you get this fine specimen of livestock."

"You know that this animal is of superior show quality. Look Sponge, at the bone, length, and height of this calf," she added.

I explained the cross-breeding program that produced the calf and also reminded them that I had told them about Marjorie starting her unique breeding program about three years ago.

I went on to tell them about the different crosses that we were fooling around with and the success that the ranch had had in providing winners at the major open steer and heifer shows.

"Through a lot of expense, persistence and determination, Marjorie's program has only gotten better and will continue to improve with the passing of time. She has a very successful plan for the future of our breeding program," I told them.

As both of them stood and continued to look at the pictures, I knew what they would want next.

Sure enough, they asked me to take them to Marjorie's and let them purchase some breeding stock from her ranch.

I looked at them, and there was not a way in the world that I would have said no to them.

"My friends, I will set it up and we will go down. I will let you know after I speak with Marjorie."

After loading Rue and all the dogs, we said goodbye to our mountain friends with a promise of a short time before we would return. I just loved playing cowboy with my hill folks.

There was a strong breeze out of the north, and I really noticed it when I turned south on Highway 259. I cranked the eight track up with George Strait playing and rode the breeze home

GOING BACK HOME

Upon arriving back home, there were a couple of days spent relaxing and getting the camper and our camping stuff situated. The fifth wheel had to be packed, filled with potable water, propane tanks filled, axles greased, and pressure in all the tires checked.

Regular service each spring included greasing the wheel bearings and wet bolts. You always want to do everything possible to avoid trouble while traveling.

After two days of buying groceries and checking off lists, we were ready to pull out. There was a receiver hitch on the back of the fifth wheel and we used it to pull our bass boat along with us to the lake.

The kids were as excited, if not more so, than we were; there were four to five days of nothing but relaxation ahead of us.

Cooking out has always been one of the best things about camping, and we were fully prepared for using the grill on most of our meals.

One day would be dedicated to catching catfish to have a fish fry and invite several of our friends who lived nearby. This was one of the highlights of our camping trips and our friends looked forward to it.

Upon completion of a great weekend, we returned home and prepared for the summer.

That summer started off with really hot weather early on. During the first week of August the weather moderated and nearly every day there was plenty of cloud cover. I was fishing Bob Sandlin regularly and found the bass nestled in the grassy areas over the long points and isolated submerged islands on the upper end.

I remember going almost every morning at daylight and fishing until the middle of the morning. At that time, I would pull out and return home, clean up and go to work.

August and September were very productive months for me, and by the middle of September I found the bass on Lake Fork in the same places as where I had been catching them on Sandlin.

Chatter baits thrown in heavy weeds, over the points, on cloudy days, did the trick for us during the day. Black, silver and white combinations worked well.

Several of my friends that found out I was slaying good fish, threw in with me and got in on the action. It was a fisherman's dream and believe it or not, we finally got tired of catching them.

Long A's and Zara Spooks worked wonders at daylight with the lightweight jigs and trailers used after the sun began hitting the water. I do not think that I will ever forget the vicious explosions we got on the Zara Spooks at daylight; the fish were definitely in a kill mood.

A TRIP TO MARJORIE'S
TO BUY BREEDING STOCK

About a day after I arrived home from Sponge and Linda's, I called Marjorie Bowles and told her that I had two friends up in the Kiamichi Mountains that saw the picture of my steer calf and wanted to come down to her ranch and pick out some breeding stock.

I explained that both of them were top quality people and had a fantastic mountain livestock operation. They were interested in getting into the show calf business and wanted her quality in their calves.

Marjorie was excited to hear from me and was excited that someone else was excited about her breeding program.

She also asked me if I was coming down for opening dove season, and I told her that I was trying to fit such a trip in. I also told her that Linda, Sponge and I might "kill two birds with one stone" and all come for opening weekend.

That would allow them time to look at all the breeding stock and possibly pick out some prospects to go north with. Marjorie loved the idea and told me to set it up.

I got on the cell phone with her on the call and set it all up for opening weekend of dove season.

When I hung up, Marjorie immediately called back, laughing, and added, "We will have a party under the live oaks with barbecue dove breasts and stuffed jalapeno poppers. We cannot let an opportunity for a party go to waste; I will start a list."

That was my Marjorie. Oh, how she loved company and entertaining.

Dove season rolled around, and Linda and Sponge came by and met at my place and we headed to the Hill Country with our gear. They were pulling Sponge's 36-foot gooseneck and I had my 24-foot hooked up.

They both spoke of how much fun it would be, shooting the dove over the milo and sunflower fields at Marjorie's.

In a pawn shop in Athens, Texas, we stopped, and Linda found a Browning Citori in a 12 gauge that she really liked. After she finished haggling with the owner, she walked out with it for $1,000. He originally had $1,350 on it when we walked in.

We also bought another case of shells and some light camouflage netting to use to better conceal us on the turn rows.

As we loaded back up in our trucks, Linda was saying, "That new Browning over and under will get a workout this weekend when the dove come to the grain fields."

The east side of Waco, we refueled and picked up Interstate 35S. From there we took the cutoff to Killeen and Lampasas and hit 281 headed south.

Linda mentioned stopping and having lunch and I told her that "Juanita will have sandwiches for us as soon as we get to the ranch, she always does."

Linda and Sponge stood it as long as they could. In Marble Falls we stopped at the Dairy Queen and had hamburgers and fries. In less than 45 minutes, we were back on the road.

It was almost 4:30 in the afternoon when we pulled across the big cattle guard and made our way to Marjorie's ranch house. As we pulled up, they were all there, waiting to greet us. It was just as I had never left.

After all the introductions, Juanita ushered us into her kitchen to find a table prepared for serving sandwiches and all the trimmings. All she had to do was retrieve the big platter from the walk-in cooler.

We ate as if we had just crossed the state of Texas without one morsel. After the sandwiches were eaten, Juanita broke out a key lime pie and we demolished that.

Juanita mentioned, "I was not planning on any supper since we knew you all would get here later in the afternoon."

"Juanita, that is just fine with us. I do not think we will need anything until in the morning when you start one of your famous breakfasts," I added.

Everyone chuckled, and we retired to the big room to visit before it was time for bed.

I sat and listened to Marjorie visit with Linda and Spongell. Their acquaintances were fairly new, and I knew that afforded just a small amount of time together. It would be like they had known each other forever.

It needed to be that way. Personally, I do not think that Marjorie would have sold them one head of livestock without feeling that she really knew them. Strange or not, there are some people like that, and in this part of the country you run across them more regularly.

I have no explanations for it. It is just one of those things about people, and it is impossible for me to explain. All I know is, that is the way some folks are, and I like it. Those type of individuals usually stand solid in many other areas.

"What time should the hunt commence in the morning and how are we going to pair up?" was Marjorie's question to all of us.

Let's go for 8:00, after Juanita's big breakfast, and we have given the dove time to leave their roost, water and start moving toward the grain fields.

Sponge said that he would hunt a fencerow with Linda and give me a chance to team up with Marjorie.

My reply was, "That is great, and Marjorie and I can spot the two of you in an ideal spot before going to our locations."

Walter and Sally agreed to hunt one of the lower tanks. There was an abundance of shade in that area, and it always attracted many dove, both early and late.

Marjorie and I took the Jeep and dropped Linda and Sponge off on a knoll that ran across the cross fence. It had proven to be an excellent location for doves in the past.

One afternoon, about three years ago, Marjorie and I stood in that exact spot and killed almost 200. We would have taken more but we ran out of high-brass shells.

Marjorie and I selected an upper tank of about three acres and set up on our stools to await their arrival. As we were walking to get into position, we noticed that there were birds in the air and they seemed to be everywhere.

As we settled in and loaded our guns, the dove moved in closer to us. We started taking passing shots and as soon as we started, we heard the report of the shotguns of the other hunters.

We had the dove stirring as they were flying between our groups which offered an abundance of morning action.

After about an hour, Marjorie and I stopped shooting and began picking up our game. It took us quite a while because of the way the doves were coming in; they were easy shots for us.

It was about noon by the time we assembled with the other hunters and counted our birds. Three groups of hunters had taken almost 400 dove that morning. The birds were large, and they were fat because of their daily access to the excellent grain fields.

When we arrived back at the ranch house, Sponge, Walter and I began cleaning our morning take.

Marjorie took the women into the house to plan the festivities of the night.

At about three o'clock the doves were all processed and were on salted ice awaiting the barbecue pit. Walter had a couple of the ranch hands gather an adequate amount of mesquite wood for me to grill the dove breasts.

About 4:30, I lighted my mesquite fires and began the charcoal making. By 6:00, the coals were ready and some of the guests had started arriving.

Cocktails were flowing freely, and Marjorie gave me the nod to start cooking the breasts over the mesquite coals. They were prepared with a strip of bacon wrapped around them and pinned with a toothpick. It usually took about 15 minutes on each side before turning the breast over the coals.

Over another bed of coals, we had prepared "jalapeno poppers" that Juanita and Sally had made up. They also had prepared fresh corn on the cob, still in the shock.

These were injected with a salt, black pepper, and butter concoction that just set them off perfectly. They were placed over the hot coals for about 30 minutes.

When the meal was ready, Marjorie called all the guests together, under the live oaks, and returned thanks for the bountiful table Juanita had presented.

The guests raved about how the taste of everything melded together to produce such a unique and delicious meal.

And yes, Marjorie had me prepare 100 Bratwurst sausages to go along with the meal, for the ones that did not care for the dove breasts. Juanita had made 100 buns for the sausages.

Sponge and Linda sat with me and Marjorie as we enjoyed our dinner in the open air under the live oaks.

A distant fiddle of Bob Wills played in the background as we sat and enjoyed the meal and each other's company.

I have looked back over the years and have thought many times about us all sitting there, laughing that evening; it was definitely happy times that left an indelible impression in my mind.

Walter spoke of the old days and how much fun the old timers must have had with their soirees. He mentioned that back then, there was never a dinner or celebration held without the fiddles and the music. Neighbors would usually end up laughing and dancing the night away.

Sally mentioned how times were so much different now and if people still conducted themselves as they did in the old days, there would be less problems in the world today. Everyone agreed with her.

I sat and listened and thought about what she was saying as she spoke. Being more traveled than the rest of the group, I thought about how fortunate the Hill Country people were to still have what they possessed. I knew in time, that too would be leaving, but for tonight they were so lucky to still maintain many of the old ways.

I always thought how lucky a man I am, thanks to my Hill Country friends, in being able to enjoy the tail end of such good times.

After the party, Sunday morning found us all relaxing and taking it easy. Juanita had prepared a light breakfast. Marjorie had announced over the meal that we would load up in the afternoon and go and see the breeding stock.

From there, the conversation turned to the breeding program, the genetic infusion that she had started several years ago and the success of all the prior planning. She brought out photos of her offspring winning all of the major open shows of the Southwest.

Sponge and Linda were much more than impressed and were anxious to go and see her stock.

By now, it was evident that Marjorie had taken to Sponge and Linda and purchasing her livestock would no longer be a problem.

After a light brunch for lunch, we loaded up in the ranch vehicles and made our way to the crossbred heifer pens. From there, we toured the three to four-year-old cow operations. When finished with that group, we looked at the older cows and their calves.

A finer bunch of cattle I have never seen, and I have been on most of the larger ranches in Texas. The crossbreeding did the trick for Marjorie.

About mid-afternoon, Marjorie told them that it was time to choose what they wanted.

After careful thought and much deliberation, Sponge told Marjorie, "We want ten Simmental cross heifers and twenty cows, three to four years old."

Marjorie reached for her paint gun behind the seat of the jeep and told them to start selecting, and she would mark what they wanted. From there, the ranch hands would cut the selected cattle out and move them to the working pens.

After three to four more hours, the cattle were selected. Marjorie remarked that they would be moved to the pens the first thing next morning. "We can settle on the price tonight, if that is okay with the two of you."

One thousand dollars each for the heifers, and $1,200 each for the "mama" cows were the agreed price, and Marjorie poured our libations to seal the deal. It was kind of a dramatic moment for all of us; I was more than happy to be part of the ceremony.

Juanita served thick steaks, baked potatoes, and all the trimmings for dinner. We finished the night with mixed cocktails before turning in. I drifted off to sleep thinking about the improvement of show quality livestock that was coming to Oklahoma. I was proud to be a part of it.

After breakfast the next morning, Sponge and I got our trailers and pulled them to the working pens. There we found the ranch vaqueros with the selected cattle, penned and ready to load for us.

We said all of our "goodbyes" at the working pens. After the hugging was over it was time to pull out. I told Marjorie that I would be back for turkey season.

"Maybe we can find some time to spend up on Juniper's Knoll, next time," I said.

Marjorie looked at me, smiled big and said, "Jim, you know how much I would like that."

Linda paid Marjorie cash money for the livestock and everything was settled. It was time for the three of us to head north. We were headed to the Kiamichi Mountains with new breeding stock for the Eubanders. There was much excitement involved from all of us.

The traffic was good on a Sunday morning. I had always found that Sundays are the best days to be on the road; there is far less traffic on those days.

By 3:00, we were back in Daingerfield and on Highway 259, headed north, toward The Winding Stair Mountains. We should be at the Rocking E by dark thirty.

Upon arrival, we unloaded the livestock into the big corral at the house. Linda checked the water troughs while Sponge and I grained the new arrivals. Surprising, they seemed settled and at home at their new home.

Linda prepared sandwiches for us, and Sponge and I showered. After we ate, we drifted into the big room and made ourselves comfortable while

Linda poured us a tad of her delicious muscadine wine. Oh, how it all came together.

After another great night of sleep, high in the Kiamichi Mountains, I was ready to return home and relax with the family for a few days.

By 2:00 Monday afternoon, I pulled into the front yard. Anita and the kids were there to greet me. It was good to be back home; the miles have taken a toll on me and I needed the rest.

A CALL FROM THE HILLS

Linda and Sponge called in about six weeks and wanted me to come up and see the crossbred cattle they had purchased from Marjorie Bowles.

I told them I would be up that way in about a week and would call the day before I came; the date was set.

Before getting off the phone, Linda had explained that they wanted me to come help them pick out the sires for next year 20-cow breeding program. The cattle had been bred to Chianina sires and would be calving within the next couple of months. They wanted to make sure we had plenty of time to select the best possible sires that we could secure semen from.

We expected the Chianina sires to produce a yellowish white offspring with spectacular size and growth ability. We also expected the first crop of calves to have many open show winning prospects.

All of this would give me plenty of information to think about before I arrived at their mountain ranch.

.   .   .

It was two weeks before I actually arrived at their ranch. Sponge and Linda were glad to see me, and the first thing we did was drive out to a long valley where the 20 crossbred cows and 10 heifers were located.

The heifers would be ready for breeding in four months, and Sponge and Linda wanted to pick out artificial insemination sires for that program; we had a lot of selecting to do, but we were allowing ourselves enough time.

First of all, we called Carnation Farms and found out when their next Artificial Insemination School was scheduled. In one month, in Tulsa, technicians from the company would be in town for a week of instruction and practical application.

There would be sessions for artificial insemination and sessions for palpation (pregnancy testing).

Linda was excited about signing up for the classes. Back in those days, Carnation would schedule the classes to fit your needs. It did not cost anything to receive the training. The only stipulation was that the receiver was expected to purchase all of their supplies from Carnation.

Carnation would give each participant a liquid nitrogen tank and other supplies to get them started. It was a great deal for the company and for the student they trained.

After we squared all of that away, it was time to get out the catalogues and slide presentations (furnished by Carnation) to aid us in our sire selections.

We made a large chart on the kitchen table and started filling in the blanks as to what the Eubanders wanted and a plan to reach their short term and long-term goals. The procedure that we utilized was very interesting.

After two days, the plans were made, and the straws of semen were reserved for a later deliver.

The next morning, we drove out and checked the crossbred stock that had been purchased from Marjorie. It was amazing how much difference there was in the cattle since they had been relocated to the foothills of The Winding Stair Mountains. The cattle could not have been in better shape. They were a model of health, and it was evident that Sponge and Linda were taking the best of care of them.

After breakfast, the next morning and after say our "goodbyes," I got in the truck and headed south for home. Before leaving, I told them that I would be back for the beginning of breeding season.

HOW WE OPENED DOVE SEASON EACH YEAR

September would bring the beginning of a new hunting season and for the folks that loved to shoot the shotguns, it was the beginning of the year.

We opened dove season just as we always did, on the sunflower fields at Throckmorton. Two to three weeks later, we would travel to a friend's ranch in San Angelo and finish out the season on a four-day hunt with a big feast every night with dove breasts cooked over mesquite coals.

We wrapped the individual breasts in bacon with a split jalapeno pepper stuffed with cheese placed in the chest cavity before it was wrapped with the bacon. After that, salt, pepper and hot mesquite coals did the trick.

Cold beer and cocktails were the choice of drinks with our meals. Local friends of the rancher and business people of the town came out to the ranch on Saturday night where there was plenty to eat and the enjoyment of a live fiddle band that performed for everyone. The Bob Wills fiddle music in the late San Angelo evening was memorable.

Teal season followed dove season, and the blinds were reconstructed on Lake Bob Sandlin and Lake of the Pines. Targeting the bombarding kamikazes would always sharpen the shooting skills of any gunner; many times, they would humble the prowess of our best shooters.

It did not take much to get the teal to buzz the blinds that were constructed on long points and a few blocks strategically placed to get their attention. They were never considered to be the smartest ducks, but their maneuverability antics were second to none. It was so much fun just being there for the show they put on.

By the time teal season was coming to an end, we would rig our lines and return to Maud, Texas and Lake Wright Patman for the best tasting channel catfish in the world.

Where did the unique taste come from? Maybe it was naturally extracted from the soil that the Sulphur River made its journey through. Inquiries have been made to the smartest woodsmen in the country, but I have never received what I thought was a satisfactory answer.

It would take us about two weeks to fill all our freezers with the delectable eating. Concluding our efforts, we would always host a huge fish fry and invite all our friends and old timers to enjoy the treat. Everyone looked forward to this occasion.

October would find us at a squirrel camp down on Big Cypress Creek and a group of us camping out for opening squirrel season. There were usually about twenty of us that would participate each fall.

With the inception of the Russian Boar in the late 1970s, the squirrel hunting began to taper off. We started experiencing too many encounters with the newcomers to the bottoms; many of them turned out not so good.

Russian Boar sows make their bed for baby pigs in the leaves and straws of the bottom. They select a spot among several saplings that are one-half inch to three-quarter inch in diameter. The sows will snap the saplings off about 14-16 inches above the ground and place them on top to

188

support vines and branches that they place on top of that.

When the females get finished with their bed, it is almost impossible to recognize it as such until it is too late. The sow can bust from under the cover and take a man down quicker than he can retreat. I have known of this happening to squirrel hunters more than once.

Thus, the explanation about the squirrel hunters tapering off as the Russian Boar became established in the bottoms.

Personally, I have walked in on sows giving birth and witnessed pigs being born without the sow attacking me. Once they start the birthing process, they are not nearly as dangerous as they are in the pre-birth mode. Not many woodsmen know this, and I have found only one other who has experienced this.

Regardless, it is always very important to use good judgment and be on the lookout for such signs of nesting. When they are in the pre-birth mode and guarding their bed, the sows become extremely dangerous.

The scientists say that the sows give birth twice a year. The old-timers, like myself, know better and have witnessed the Russian female raising at least three litters a year while being held in captivity.

That is the reason it is impossible to kill them out; they are much too prolific.

The experts are quick to call them feral hogs or domesticated hogs that got loose and became wild. The Russian Boar are none of the above.

The Russian has a true characteristic in having a straight tail with no curl in it. If the hog has a curl, it is not 100% Russian.

I always remarked that a herd of them in the open and from a distance appeared as if they were miniature buffalo.

I chuckled to myself when I read what the professionals say about our hogs. I never argue with them; they are the ones that have been to college and have studied such things. I just let them go on with their explanations when I encounter them at seminars. It would be embarrassing to correct them while they are, supposedly, within their element.

The ones that write about them are worse, and in their articles, they often tempt me into writing or calling them. I have found that if I just bite my tongue, in a few days the feelings that their ignorance brings passes on.

When we were at squirrel camp, it was always a great friend and family time. When we broke camp at the end of ten days, we made sure we had plenty of wood chopped and other supplies laid in that we would need during cold weather when we came back to walk the creeks and jump shoot the large greenheads that laid up out of the wind and ate acorns.

A rule of thumb was: With an abundance of lake shooting, the creeks in the bottoms would be loaded with mallards. The pressure from the lakes ran them to quieter and safer places out of the wind; thus, the bottoms were very productive, especially if it was only near freezing, the acorns were floating, and the water was still moving in the creeks. This all set the stage for jump-shooting at its best.

About a week before duck camp, we would take a portable hog trap down, place it in proximity of the campground and start baiting it with corn. By the time duck camp got in full swing we would have two or three "shoats" to butcher and either smoke or barbecue.

We cooked a brisket for one meal, and the rest of the time we were eating our pork and fried duck breasts that were filleted for the occasion. Just poor boys, living like kings, in Big Cypress Creek Bottom.

MY BROTHER BOB

It was almost dark one summer evening and my brother, Bob, called and told me that he had been asked to do some landscaping over on Lake Cypress Springs. Knowing my background, he asked me for my assistance in working up some of these estimates for his company.

The next morning, he picked me up early and we left out for pre-arranged appointments on Lake Cypress Springs.

Many of the people building, buying, and moving out on the lake are from the Dallas/Ft. Worth area, and many of them have a large income. In many cases, money is not the object when it comes to buying services that the individual really wants.

High dollar design and a complete installation can run as much as $40,000-$150,000 per project. That does include complete sodding, sprinkler system installation, and lighting as part of the turn-key job.

Boat house and pier construction is a complete other entity and can run into the hundreds of thousands dependent on how elaborate the property owner wants to go.

As all the expenses are added up, it is not difficult to exceed a million dollars, and there are several worth several million dollars.

Landscape design and installation can become a very lucrative business for the companies that have the knowledge and staff to complete some of the enormous projects.

This story leads to Bob asking me on the drive over to Cypress Springs about selecting a lakefront lot and what makes one better than another. This is the list of things that I advised him to look for when advising prospective property owners. As far as I know, the information that I offered paid off for him many times.

SELECTING LAKEFRONT PROPERTY

Knowing that I had quite a bit of experience with soils, topography and lakefront lots, my brother, Bob, asked me one time what to look for in selecting lots on the water.

After giving it much thought, I made a check-off list for selecting a desirable lakefront property.

Never purchase a lot that is next to a public boat ramp; the property will not appreciate in value. You will never be happy with the location of the lot. There will be late night noise and music from boaters entering and exiting the lake. These lots are usually reduced in price and are very attractive to prospective buyers who do not know any better.

The most ideal property is located in a deep cove away from prevailing north winds. The north wind causes most of the erosion problems that are associated with the loss of property along the water's edge.

The properties that rate as the worst are the southern bank facing north with deep exposed water in front of it. The prevailing north wind will slowly erode the lot away; lakefront real estate is way too expensive to watch it fall off into the lake.

I had a friend on Lake Bob Sandlin that had a beautiful home and a lot that was situated like this. During the first twenty years, he built two concrete seawalls, and each time it cost in excess of $125,000.

He finally decided on trying the vertical metal panels that interlock as they are driven into place. These work, provided they are long enough to drive deep below the surface of the water. They have them now that can be driven down and another one attached to it to go even deeper.

I have operated a Gradall and have sunk many of them while working on different seawall projects. This is the only way to build seawalls that will last. If anyone tries to sell you on any other idea, you should beware. They are expensive, but when it is complete, the seawall can be forgotten.

My friend with the concrete seawalls kept anchoring them deeper into the soil, but eventually the water would tunnel under and erode the soil from the back. The seawall eventually would collapse and slough off into the water.

The metal panels ended all of that, and that is all that Bob would use on his seawall construction. If the owner would approve it, Bob would use the same panels on the sides of his boathouses. That would stop any future erosion that might start major problems.

My favorite lake lot selections come from deep coves with moderate elevations down to the lake. When positioned like this they can be developed and landscaped reasonably. When a lakefront property is purchased, most owners have no idea what is in store for them; the work and the expense are never-ending.

It is an excellent idea to look for a deeper lot instead of a wide one. The more of the lot bordering the waterfront, the more expensive it is to maintain. Where land touches water is the area of highest concern.

Potential buyers should stay away from shallow coves. The water levels fluctuate too much, and during the best time of the year to enjoy water sports, you are dry docked. I had a friend one time that built a very expensive home in the back end of a shallow cove.

He eventually got a huge dredging machine to come in and cut a channel from the main lake to his boathouse. The channel ended up over a one-quarter mile long, and after about three years the channel had silted in again.

Do not depend on real estate brokers to make you aware of the trials and tribulations that can await you. Most of them do not know and are interested in only one thing: their commission.

One needed improvement leads to another one that must be done to accommodate the first one; it is never-ending. It is mandatory that property owners have access to plenty of money when they are developing lake lots and building their home on the lake.

I have known a few people who lived on the lake that really could not afford to live on the lake. In time, they came to realize it.

I have been amazed, down through the years, by just observing and watching people waste money around their lakefront property.

If an individual is serious about purchasing lakefront property, it would repay them many times over to spend time with a knowledgeable person and walk the prospective property with that person before they purchase.

If you have not read my third book, *From A Duck Blind On Caddo Also*, pick up a copy and meet some of the property owners we did work for and the individual projects we created on beautiful Lake Fork. It describes not only the people and their homes and improvements, it talks about my thirty-five years of hunting and fishing on that lake and many of the different techniques that was used to catch fish, alligators, and also how we successfully hunted the waterfowl from our blinds and from an airboat.

The people were most interesting and remain friends of mine until this day. There are many pleasant memories left there on the water and the shorelines.

Bob had a natural instinct for creating some very beautiful landscapes for his customers, and I helped him with putting finish touches on his work.

June 4, 2010 was the day that it all came to an end. We were building a seawall on Lake Cypress Springs when my brother, Bob, suffered a massive heart attack, and within a few minutes he was gone. It was the saddest day in my life, seeing my baby brother leave this world and there was nothing I could do to prevent it.

Bob was only 51 years old and was my junior by 11 years. I miss him dearly to this day.

He was partially instrumental in encouraging me to publish my writings.

.   .   .

Before I decided to publish my stories, I spent part of a career in educational administration. I moved into that field after being an agriculture teacher in Pittsburg, Texas for ten and a half years.

I loved every day of being the agriculture teacher of a small agricultural community. My students and I were called on to do many service-oriented jobs for the small town in Northeast Texas.

Our participation and the events we were involved in are too numerous to mention, and you would not believe the contributions we made to our little town.

To this day, I am occasionally reminded of something my students did for the community or for someone. Our service to the little town was very fulfilling.

After ten and a half years as agriculture teacher at Pittsburg High School, I had an opportunity to join a group of investors and develop an oil-field supplier manufacturing facility.

Six years were spent in that industry, and it was nothing but hard work. The paycheck was much better than teaching, but it was almost a twenty-four hour a day job.

Eventually, I was hired as the CEO of the company, and my obligations to the business only intensified. It did not take me long, burning the candle at both ends, to decide to get out and attempt to regain my health and sanity in different endeavors.

I spent a couple of years in the landscaping business with my brother, Bob. That was very interesting and provided me a chance to slow down for a while.

After two years, I returned to education and took a job at Texas High School in Texarkana, Texas.

As I was fulfilling my work assignments, I would attend college classes in the evening at Texas A&M – Texarkana. I enrolled and began my studies in secondary education.

The courses came easy to me because I was a little older now and with the ten and one-half years of teaching experience, the liberal application of common sense and past experiences allowed me to be successful.

After receiving my secondary education and superintendent certifications, I began applying what I had learned.

First, I took a job as high school principal at Whitesboro, Texas. My family and I spent three years in that wonderful community and enjoyed every minute of it. I would have probably stayed but the board hired a superintendent that was "nuts." Too many times, I have seen that happen to school districts.

From there, I left Whitesboro High School after we successfully passed a bond issue, and I was instrumental in helping build the new high school located on the south side of Highway 82, as you pass through the community.

My family and I moved to Yantis, Texas as I accepted a superintendent's position and worked in that capacity for four years or until I reached the age and experience total number that allowed me to retire.

Upon retirement, Anita and I moved back to Pittsburg, Texas and built our retirement home on our acreage at a small rural community once known as Faker Switch, because of the train switching track at that location.

We had our acreage and a large garden of about three-fourths of an acre. There, I raised everything you can think of. We had sweet corn, Brussels sprouts, broccoli, carrots, peppers, onions, an assortment of greens, cabbage, Irish potatoes and sweet potatoes, sugar cane, field corn, peas, beans, onions, watermelons, cantaloupes, peaches, strawberries, collards, all varieties of tomatoes, tomatillos, all varieties of squash, peanuts, a row of cotton, a row of tobacco and several other plants of interests.

My plants were all irrigated with drip lines, and I had acquired implements to mechanically work and till the garden.

Full-time work was an understatement, but it was thoroughly enjoyable to watch the plants grow and the produce mature. There was food for many of my friends and neighbors.

It saddened me greatly when I realized that many folks we invited to come out and pick their fill would decline our offer.

BACK TO WORK

After being retired for about two months, I received a call from Pittsburg Independent School District and was asked to come back and reinstate discipline in the high school.

The offer enticed me because it allowed me to make two paychecks. I would continue to receive my monthly retirement check and an additional check from Pittsburg ISD.

It did not take long to gain the respect from the students and get things moving in the right direction. The accomplishment came easy to me because of my past experiences dealing with students and parents. I really enjoyed seeing everything come together.

After two or three years, some of the board members began lending a sympathetic ear and responding to the parents of students that I had to come down extra hard on. This was something that they promised they would not do when I was employed for the job. I was to have free reign and the resources for cleaning up the discipline and implementing new proven programs for the high school students.

After the parental pressure was applied to some of the weaker school board members, it carried over to the superintendent who had a tendency to go either way. I recognized immediately that my days of moving the school forward were fast coming to an end.

At the end of five years, I hung it up for the second time and went back to our retirement home at Faker. Anita kept teaching, and I spent my days with my dogs, on the farm doing what we loved to do. That consisted mostly of riding in the bottoms on the Kubota, hunting, fishing and gardening.

I set lines on the creek after the good rains and kept my hog traps baited. I had a friend that was a butcher at Safeway, and he processed everything that we caught or killed. There was always fresh meat for the grill, and it remained hot most of the time.

There we lived and were very happy until the summer of 2018. Anita and I decided that there was just too much to see after on the farm, and we needed a smaller place. We started looking for such and were led down to Holly Lake Ranch, west of Gilmer, Texas on Highway 154 and near Hawkins, Texas on Highway 2869.

Our new home is in a gated community with about 3,500 other residents. We have a nice home and lot within the development, and I have daily access to a really nice and challenging golf course; things are really great at the Ranch.

When the weather permits, and that is almost every day, I play golf with a group of friends.

I get out of bed every morning about 5:00 a.m. and after having my coffee and checking my emails, I check my Facebook pages for book sales and conduct that business before I spend at least two hours a day in my office, with my writing.

At about 11:00 a.m., I get on my golf cart and go down to the pro shop to hit balls and practice putt before my afternoon round. Life is great at the Ranch.

While not sitting at the computer and writing, I find myself with an adequate amount of time to do my contemplating and I do my share of it about the old days, old friends, old lessons, old dogs and old memories of the past.

Most of my contemplation is very enjoyable, and occasionally I stop and ask myself if I would do anything differently if the chance presented itself for me to relive my life. I must admit that there are some things that I would change if I had a redo, but most of my life, I would not change very much. It has been a good run.

Particular incidents slip back in my mind during times of contemplations. I have notated the following as one of the more entertaining:

AN INTERVIEW ON THE COAST

During my career as a school administrator, I was known as a fair man among the majority of parents and students and an enforcer of a strict code of discipline.

I loved my students and protecting them was my foremost thought. When the student arrived at school each morning, I felt as if it was my responsibility to take care of their needs and protect them until they returned to their home and parents in the afternoon. In return, I expected every student to respect the adults and their fellow students on campus and always be on their best behavior.

It did not take long for word to get around about my expectations for student success. I was an assistant principal at a fairly large Northeast Texas high school. During my five years at that school, I took up eight handguns from troubled students and luckily not one of them resisted. I always felt as if my rapport with the student body allowed me to safely accomplish this.

I was present during two drive-by shootings and witnessed much gang activity during my tenure at that school. My experience with difficult students and campuses prepared me to share my information with other school districts.

I was called upon and was involved with establishing school police departments in three different school districts in my earlier years. That was a time when most school districts had not even heard of a police department within their school.

One afternoon, I was contacted by a large high school in a coastal city. The call surprised me, and it was in reference to the possibility of me flying down and interviewing for the position of principal of their school.

My name had been referred by an executive director of one of the state's education service centers. She had previously worked with me and gave them my name and phone number with a note, "he is your man."

I made arrangements for the trip and to meet with the selection team at the school, along with scheduling an appointment for such a meeting. I was interested in the position because: It was obvious that they needed help, the job would be a great challenge, and it paid a huge salary. I knew that my expertise would assist me in being successful with the job.

The day arrived, and they picked me up at the airport. I walked into the meeting room with about one hundred school administrators, board members, business people, students, teachers and parents of that school district and city.

Introductions took about thirty minutes, and then I was called upon to explain my philosophy of education to the group during my opening remarks.

I had done extensive research on the school and molded my address to mesh with their needs. I knew from my personal study that their high school had eighteen different ethnic groups or cultures that represented countries from all over the world. Their overall test scores were very low, teacher turnover was ridiculous, gangs and drugs were prevalent, the number of student dropouts was growing and their graduation rates for the past several years had steadily been declining.

My research also revealed that the school had been plagued year after year with extreme violence. There had been two murders on campus within the last year. Many gang related incidents had been reported, and there had been six rapes on campus during the last ten months; a teacher's car had been burned along with the art complex.

To put it lightly, the school was a "hell hole." They did not need a principal as much as the school needed a company of Texas Rangers.

During the last four years, there had been eight different principals hired and they had all left or been fired.

It did not take a rocket scientist to know that the school had huge problems, and it was going to take an individual with the know-how to come in and completely retool the administrative management structure of the campus. A discipline matrix for the campus had to be designed to fit the needs of that campus. Most importantly, it was going to take support from the district superintendent and especially the school board members. In many situations, that is where the link is broken.

To be successful, it takes a complete "buy-in" from all the participants. Everyone has to work together for common goals. It was not going to be easy. The school, the students, the parents and community had to be retooled along with their way of thinking, to achieve successful results. A major paradigm shift was in order, and to be successful there were no short cuts around it.

As I spoke to the group, I reiterated the need for change, the new paradigms, and the definite requirement for discipline and how it must be applied. I stressed goal setting, student involvement, parent involvement and teamwork to accomplish those goals. A combination of all participants had to own the new plan for it to work.

After a lengthy discussion and fielding many questions from the attendants at the interview, the same question kept presenting itself, "Mr. Richardson, do you think that you can institute the change that you speak of?"

My reply was, "Yes, provided that I am equipped with the proper tools to perform the task and if the central administration and board members will commit to our goals and stand behind them."

I told the group that things would get worse before they got better. I also made the comment that within six-weeks a positive change would be seen, and in six-months to a year, we would be near where we needed to be.

The campus enrollment was forty-six hundred students, and I pointed out to the interviewers that it would be necessary to establish a school police force. We would need a police chief and eight to ten uniformed officers for our campus alone.

Expanding the vocational curriculum to include offering many chances for students to gain meaningful employment upon graduation was stressed.

If I was employed, we would need to develop an alternative education program with certified teachers that taught a curriculum similar to the one that was taught on the main campus. There also would be a credit recovery program developed, and all credits would apply toward an alternative education graduation certificate.

I requested six first-assistant vice-principals and eight assistant principals as my administrators, of which the majority would be bi-lingual and fluent in several different languages.

Out of the corner of my eye, I could see the business manager of the school district squirming and running the numbers as I spoke. At one time, he stopped me and asked me if I knew what kind of dollars were being proposed. I replied to him that I did know and mentioned a figure to him that seemed to answer his question.

I continued until I had finished with what I wanted to say, and then the question came again, "Mr. Richardson, do you really think that you can institute the change that you speak of?"

Once again, I told the group that there was no doubt in my mind. If I was provided with the resources and if the superintendent and school board members would stand behind me, support our changes and not run backward from parent and community pressures, it could be accomplished.

I went on to explain to the group that resisting parental pressure is the hardest battle in standing behind campus administration. In most communities, parental pressure, applied through school board members, is the main deterrent to consistency; consistency is the mainstay for any worthwhile organization. A school either has it or it doesn't. There are no in-betweens.

After about two hours, they thanked me for attending and dismissed me from the meeting. On my way to the main entrance of the room, I stopped, turned, and shared one last thing with the group.

"Don't misunderstand me, I do know that you want a safe school, and I know that you want a good school. Those are my wants, also. We have spoken of some really beneficial changes this afternoon and the magnitude of those changes may sound as if they are overwhelming to you at first. I know that all of you will need some time to mull such ideas over."

The last remark that I will leave you with is, "If you do not really want what we have spoken of, do not ask for it. If you do not really want what you have heard, I am not your man."

If you select me as your new principal, I will bring what you ask for, provided I have the continued support of the stakeholders. As long as I possess that, we will move forward as a campus and a school district.

To make a long story shorter, I was not offered the job down on the coast.

About three months later, I ran into two of the interviewers at an administrators' meeting during a national conference in Kansas City. They recognized me and approached me and introduced themselves once again. We visited for a while, and I asked them about who they had employed to fill their position.

They told me the committee had decided on a lady from California who had great credentials and had wonderful answers to all the questions and everyone just loved her. She had her Ed. D. and Ph. D. and had done tons of research in troubled student areas and had written at length about it.

I just had to ask, "How is she working out for you?"

They told me that she had already gone back to California during the first six-weeks of her tenure. One of the assistant principals was filling in until they could get the committee back together and round up some applicants to interview for another campus principal.

"Would you come back for another interview?" they asked.

I told them that I did not think that I would be interested in doing that.

I went on to say, "I guess all the additional resources that I asked for was going to cost the district too much money?"

They both said it was not that. They went on to inform me that I stood in favor with most of the interview team until I said, "if you do not really want it, don't ask for it."

They went on to explain that it was that particular remark that frightened some members of the interview group.

I shook their hand, bid them farewell, turned, and while chuckling under my breath, walked away.

In retirement, I have had much time to contemplate the interview at the large high school down on the coast.

Sometimes that contemplation causes me to ponder the question of whether our students are the real problems with America's schools.

My past experience tells me that in many cases, the answer is "no."

It is often the school board members that we have elected and the adults that we have employed and placed in charge that have failed us. Most of them are too engrained in a failing system and are too busy trying to please parents and build a retirement fund rather than serving students.

That same high school is in search of a principal today.

ENVIRONMENTAL SAFETY

Leaving the farm and moving into a more environmentally safe-minded culture and neighborhood at Holly Lake Ranch, I have found and recommend the following safe weed and grass killing procedures to my friends.

You can never be too safe when dealing with chemicals; most of them never completely dissipate and potentially one day will get back into our food or water supply.

I am personally convinced that process is slowly happening now. Results of it appear occasionally, and some of us who know what we are looking for recognize it as such.

There are many concerns lately with using weed killers. I discovered a mixture that does a fantastic job in elimination of grass and weed growth in areas where that growth it is not wanted.

It is perfect for spraying around fences and established plants to form a "kill zone" to work up to with the weed eater or lawn mower.

The mixture is as follows:

- 1 Gallon Vinegar
- 1½ Cups Epsom Salts
- 2 tablespoons of Dawn dishwashing liquid

Mix thoroughly and fill your hand sprayer to make an effective application of the ingredients for the control of grass and weeds.

MARJORIE CALLS FROM THE HILL COUNTRY

I had just come in from a two-day bass tournament on Lake Palestine and was eating dinner with my family. Anita had prepared a wonderful meal, and the kids were catching me up on what I had missed in my absence.

In my study, after dinner, the phone rang and when I answered I was delightfully surprised that it was my friend, Marjorie Bowles, from the Texas Hill Country.

She called to tell me that it was calf working time on her place next week, and all the bull calves from the F1 females needed to be castrated, vaccinated and branded. She asked if I wanted to assist.

I always get excited when I have an opportunity to cowboy, to really cowboy again, in a world where it is becoming a dying art.

I told Marjorie that I would load Buck the following Monday and be at her ranch first thing Tuesday for the beginning of her Spring Roundup.

I had been there on two other occasions and the hard work was well rewarded by the food and nightly entertainment at her ranch house. Marjorie did love to entertain her friends.

I checked in early Tuesday morning and with Walter's assistance, stored my gear in the bunkhouse with his stuff. He then poured me a cup of coffee, and we sat down in the tack room and visited about the plans for the rest of the week.

"Jim," he said, "you know why we are starting the roundup on Wednesday morning, don't you?

"I have no idea, Walter," was my reply.

"She was not going to start until you could get here. She mentioned to me and Juanita a couple of weeks back that there would not be any more Spring Roundups without Jim here."

I thought about his statement long and hard and deep inside I swelled with pride, to think that she thought that much of our friendship. Our love for each other was true.

We had no longer than sat down for supper in the dining room when Marjorie mentioned to me that there was a big cat killing her baby goats.

"After dinner," she continued, "I will show you the cat's track from two nights ago."

The topic of Spring Roundup veered toward the cat tracks and the disappearance of the young goats.

The conversation for the rest of the meal was along the lines of cat sightings, other small animal disappearances, trapping, trailing and destroying the varmints.

Later, on the front porch, as we sat and took our regular libations of dry carrot wine, Marjorie asked if I might bring my dogs down and find the critter.

In a cloud of rich Cuban cigar smoke, I looked up from under the brim of my hat and nodded to her that it might all be possible after we had completed the Spring Roundup.

"We will work the cattle and calves, and before I leave to return home I will take Buck and look for further sign of which direction the cat or cats might be coming in from," I told her.

"The Walkers Ranch, just south of us, has 20,000 acres, and all I have to do is go by and see Gerald and you will have access to all of that range for your tracking," Marjorie added.

There was nothing else discussed about the cats that night as we all retired and went to bed; it was known that coffee time would come early at Marjorie's spread.

Coffee and breakfast was served at the usual time of 5:00 a.m. Everyone was present for the meal and in great spirits to start the exciting day of real ranch work.

There was a huge spreading live oak that covered the rear of the house and most of the backyard. It had to be old enough to have been quite a tree even when Travis, Crockett, Bowie and the other brave men of the Alamo were fighting for Texas freedom, just down the road at San Antonio de Bexar.

We all had sat around it and talked about how old it might be many times in the past. Three hundred and fifty years was a reasonable guess for its age.

"Can you imagine what the old tree has seen in its day?" was always the question posed as we sat and enjoyed the shade that it offered.

The conquistadors, the Lipan, the Comanche, had all seen it grow old.

Many of the socials that Marjorie held at the ranch was under the spreading branches of the magnificent live oak.

Rounding up and working cattle goes back many years ago on the ranches and spreads of early day cow times in Texas. It was an inherited tradition that was passed forward with each generation of cattlemen from the early days to the present. Being part of such doings was a personal connection with the early days of Texas ranching. Just being asked to come and be part of it was enough said.

As soon as we had finished breakfast, it was getting light enough to see our way around as we caught our horses from the stock remuda and saddled them for the day's work.

Buck was ready to go and sensed that we were going to be able to be cowboys again for a while.

Marjorie, Walter and I met up with six of the ranch hands and made out way by horseback to a pasture that was about a mile away. We opened gates and arranged for the planned movement as we worked our way to that particular pasture.

Walter and Marjorie had designed working lanes to move cattle from one pasture of the ranch to the other, and they sure came in handy when it came time to work the livestock.

The plan was to move the herd down the working lane and back toward the main pens near the ranch house. There, in the main working pens, was all the equipment that we would need to complete our tasks.

Upon arrival at the pasture we were looking for, the ranch hands began moving around and behind a herd of about 500 head of grown cows and their calves.

All the herd bulls had already been pulled from the herd because all the mother cows had bred back for the next calf crop. Our mission today was to pull the calves, vaccinate them, castrate, ear tag each one, spray for insects, brand each one, paste worm, and ready the worked males to put on summer wheat pasture for weight gain.

After 90 days of weight gain, they would be near 1,000 pounds each and ready for market.

During this time when we were working the male calves, there were always several high school students and vocational agriculture teachers that would come out and select steer calves for the fall livestock shows. Students of those same teachers won many times at the local shows, and more than their fair share of the big wins came with Marjorie's steers.

As we would castrate the calves, we would fill long sleeve plastic gloves with the testicles. When one glove was full it would be tied off and placed in a large cooler full of ice.

At the end of the day we might have as many as 200 testicles that would be processed and cooked for an assortment of cookouts and other entertaining events. More than once, we prepared them for large cookouts where Marjorie would invite all of her friends from the surrounding area.

And yes, the fiddle player from San Antonio was always there to play for the events. Her performances under the spreading live oak were the highlights of the gatherings.

Often, when I think about those grand times, I can close my eyes and hear her playing the beautiful music. The music drifted through the Hill Country air and off toward the majestic stream at the foot of the hills overlooking the river.

On the second night of the round-up, Marjorie instructed Juanita to make ready for another gathering of guests.

She asked Walter and me to fry up a batch of mountain scallops, French fries, and hush puppies as she and Juanita would prepare all the trimmings to go along with our doings. Gosh, it was grand.

There would usually be about 65 to 70 guests at Marjorie's parties. Everything was always just perfect; Marjorie saw to that.

This get together was no different than the many I had made in the past, and everyone seemed to have a ball as they drank their cocktails and consumed the delicacies.

We partied on into the wee hours, but everyone was in the kitchen for breakfast early the next morning and ready for another day in the working pens.

Juanita would bring cold food down to the working pens for lunch as we would all take a break and dine under the live oaks. Her fresh-squeezed lemonade was as good as any I ever tasted, and everyone loved it. It stands out in my memory today.

Sliced hoop cheese, bologna, and pickle loaf, fresh cut from the meat market in Blanco were ideal for quick sandwiches during our noon break. Large sliced sweet onions, lettuce and tomatoes on hot homemade buns set the meal off perfectly.

Juanita made a special relish dressing to go on the sandwiches. I have never tasted any like it before or since eating hers. It was absolutely delicious.

Marjorie enjoyed calling her get-togethers, a soiree. Her soirees always involved great food and drink.

Soiree - an evening party or gathering, typically in a private house, for conversation or music.

That night, Walter and I were talking about keeping mosquitoes away from your commons area, especially when you were having guests for a party.

The next morning, Walter broke out a Paul Harvey recipe for a yard spray around the house. He gave me a copy, and I included it here. It works.

Paul Harvey Yard Spray

1 bottle of blue mint mouthwash
3 bottles (per 12 oz.) of stale beer (take the cheapest – it works as well)
3 cups of Epsom salt

Mix this up and make sure the salt dissolves. Put in your Ace Sprayer and spray your flower beds and around the patio. He didn't have mosquitos for 90 days last summer!

Walter also asked me if we were to trail the cats to determine their trails to and away from the ranch. I told him that we would saddle up and begin our trek to see where it might take us.

By noon, we had discovered a definite trail of movement coming in due south of the ranch. About 10 miles after leaving Marjorie's and entering her neighbor's land, we found a gentle rise of foothills.

We found a den in the side of one of the hills after about another of riding. We also discovered some older bones and residue that made it evident that we had found where they slept.

"Walter, we will need Cortez and the Ridgebacks to finish this job," I told him. "When I get back home, I will load our gear and make plans to return and hunt the cats with you."

I pulled out from the ranch early the next morning, headed home. I had a busy week before me, but with all good breaks, maybe I could be headed south again by Friday at noon.

KEY LIME POUND CAKE

I can hardly remember going to Marjorie's that Juanita did not have a Key Lime Pound Cake sitting under glass on an all-glass pedestal on the center island, in the main kitchen.

This was another one of "Juanita's Delights" that came to mind this morning when I was going through some old recipes that she had given me back in the 1980s.

Thumbing through them, I found myself stopping several times and reminiscing about the day she had given me her copy. Before I knew it, I had spent almost three hours with my friends again, even after all these years.

Memories, I know of nothing sweeter; it is such a personal treat to recall such times and enjoy each one of them again. It is a truly blessed person who has the ability to do this.

This pound cake recipe caught my eye as I was wandering back over time spent with my friends, many years ago, in the Texas Hill Country. Copy it and keep it. Do not lose it. Prepare it for your loved ones, and I assure you it will make memories for them to cherish someday.

KEY LIME POUND CAKE
WITH KEY LIME CREAM CHEESE ICING

- 4 sticks butter, that's 1 pound, room temperature
- 3 cups sugar
- 6 large eggs, room temperature
- 4 cups all-purpose flour
- $1/2$ cup fresh key lime juice
- $1/4$ cup evaporated milk, (I always keep a good number of those small, 5-ounce cans in my pantry.)
- 4 teaspoons key lime zest, minced

- 1 teaspoon vanilla

1. Preheat oven to 300°. Cover inside of 10-inch tube pan with non-stick spray. My pan is 10$^1/_2$″ and it's just fine. Set aside.
2. Using a stand-up mixer or electric hand-held, beat the butter well until light in color and fluffy. Add the sugar and again beat well for at least 5 minutes. I use a stand-up mixer and beat the mixture 10-15 minutes. I don't like a "grainy" cake.
3. One at a time, add the eggs and beat only until the yellow disappears.
4. Stir juice, milk, zest and vanilla together.
5. Now mixing by hand, gradually add flour to the butter-egg mixture alternating with the key lime juice and milk mixture. Begin and end with flour. Mix well but just enough to incorporate all ingredients. You don't want a tough pound cake!
6. Pour evenly into the tube pan and tap pan on the counter to loosen any air bubbles.
7. Bake for 1 hour and 45 minutes or until cake tester comes out clean.
8. Cool on a cooling rack for 20-25 minutes in the pan then transfer from pan to cooling rack and allow to cool another hour or until completely cool.

The cake is far better the following day or two days later.

Key Lime Cream Cheese Icing

- 8 ounces of cream cheese, room temperature
- 3-4 tablespoons butter, room temperature
- 4 cups confectioner's sugar
- $1/4$ cup freshly squeezed key lime juice
- 2-3 teaspoons key lime zest
- 1 teaspoon vanilla extract

1. Using a hand mixer beat cream cheese and butter in a large bowl until well mixed.
2. Add confectioner's sugar and beat well until completely smooth and fluffy.
3. Add key lime juice, zest and vanilla and mix until all ingredients are incorporated.
4. Ice cake.

This makes quite a bit of icing. After icing the entire pound cake, fill the middle hole with the excess icing. When the cake is served, icing can be taken from the middle and dolloped along the side the slice of cake.

A RETURN TO MARJORIE'S
TO HUNT THE CATS

Toward the end of the week, maybe Thursday night, I got around to packing for the mountain lion hunt at Marjorie's. My plans were to leave out Friday about noon and roll in down there before dark thirty.

Buck, Cortez and the Ridgebacks rolled south with me. I wanted to take them and Walter and find the cats that we cut sign on the previous weekend.

A little short of noon on Friday, we all pulled out, headed to the Hill Country. I think Buck and the dogs were as excited as I was to finally be rolling. Sometimes the getting ready and packing part can wear you out. Other times, getting ready and the anticipation of what lies ahead is all part of the trip.

At Waco, I stopped and refueled. From there, we made our way to Lampasas where we stopped at a famous family diner and had a late lunch. The owner always had meat scraps for my dogs, and when coming back through I usually had game for his cooler. There is no telling how much bartering we did through the years.

We all rolled in to the main gate at Marjorie's a short time before dark. As always, the group was gathered and waiting under the live oaks for our return.

After short salutations, Walter helped me unload the trailer and we put all of the animals in the barn for the night. I fed the dogs while Walter grained Buck. Like humans, traveling takes its toll on animals, and they need the rest as much as we do.

Upon entering the ranch house, Juanita had sandwiches, iced sweet tea, cheese slices, pickled apple rings and homemade potato chips for dinner. Nothing could have been better after the drive down.

After our meal, we all retired to Marjorie's big room while Sally poured up the first of our libations for the night. With each pour, they only got better.

Marjorie mentioned a story and wanted me to retell them to the group. First, was the fishing one about the pair of eleven-pound bass that we caught out of Lake Fork, just before a violent storm moved down the lake.

The second story she wanted to hear was about my friend, Ray Price, and the time we spent together, fishing.

A hush fell across the room as I pulled a copy of the stories from my briefcase and began to read.

A PAIR OF ELEVENS

Back during the 80s when I was really serious about chasing the sow bass, the fishing rig stayed hooked up to the Blazer 24/7. The batteries were kept hot and ready to go.

To be successful, it was important to watch the weather and try to fish in front of the severe weather changes. February would bring one of the desired changes about every 7 to 10 days. February was the month that brought the big fish for me.

Before turning in every night, the last thing to do was get a current weather report and determine if a front was moving into our area.

It was not uncommon to set an alarm for 1 or 2 in the morning in order to get up and get to a predetermined spot at least an hour before the weather change.

So was the night when I planned to be on Coffee Creek at Lake Fork at 4:30 in front of the storm. Earlier in the week there had been a large fish that took my jig and started moving out of the creek with it.

I set the hook, but it must have been perfect to have missed her. The hook never touched her and later in the morning when we graphed that area two really nice fish showed up. They were on the inside bend of the creek between several big stumps.

Twelve feet of water next to a seven-foot drop-off was an ideal location for a real line stretcher.

We left them undisturbed and moved on down the creek toward the marina to continue our outing. Several other good ones were detected along the creek before we fished out and loaded the boat.

But tonight, we were there to try our luck again.

The boat was put in at the marina about 4:00, and we started moving along the creek toward the dam. It was a good sign when I noticed there were no other boats in sight.

No one was at the marina when we unloaded, and there was very little traffic on the road. Most of the big fish seekers were still wearing out Monticello, and it was a bit early for them to be on Lake Fork.

It was also early Tuesday morning, and how many fishermen are free to go at random in front of an approaching storm?

As we trolled toward our position on the creek there was distant lightning moving from the direction of the front. It would only be a matter of time before it hit.

By 4:30 we had moved to the general area of the creek that we wanted to fish. The boat was positioned to fish toward the storm with as little help from the trolling motor as possible.

It is also important to keep the shadow of the boat off the fish. Yes, there is a shadow cast from the moon. On a completely overcast night, a 12-inch black worm can be thrown in 15 feet of water and the bass can not only hear it but see it.

It is important to be as quiet as possible because the big sows are heavy laden with eggs and are very temperamental; they are ready to fight when stuck.

All of this was taken into consideration as we readied ourselves for the first casts.

Many times, the first cast or two are the most important ones. This morning that was not the case as we continued to throw our jigs along the banks and drag them off into the creek.

A black and blue jig with a 7-inch Jaw-Tech lizard for a trailer was the bait of choice, and we were hoping it was the choice of the big bass we were after.

As we continued to cast and retrieve, we noticed the lightning intensifying as it was getting closer. It looked as if it was still 4 or 5 miles away, and we determined that we had about thirty more minutes before it hit.

At 5:15 we knew it would be here shortly. All of a sudden, my line began moving away from the creek as I stood up and set the hook hard. She was stuck, and her head was turned back toward me as the fight was on.

After a while she came up, rolled over on her side, and we slipped a dip net under her. She was immediately placed in the live well and as she went in it was easy to determine that she was a good one.

The next cast went back to the same area with no results. On the second cast after catching the big fish, the same thing happened again. The hook was set, and the fight was on again.

This fish did not put up as much fight, and as we netted her it was determined that we had to seek cover. The storm had arrived and rotten trees still standing along the creek began to fall from the strong wind.

The big engine was cranked, and we made it back to the bridge at the marina. There we waited out the storm with a big bass in the front live well and one in the back.

It took approximately an hour for the storm to finally blow through. By then the man at the marina had opened his doors and a pot of coffee was on. We loaded the boat and took the fish in to weigh.

We had an 11-pound 6-ounce and an 11-pound, 8-ounce. They were caught out of the same hole within 2 or 3 minutes of each other as the storm hit.

Eleven-pound bass are scarce, and these were the first eleven's that I had ever caught. Both were big and healthy, and we got some good pictures of the two fish.

The man at the marina took a Polaroid picture and hung it on the wall. Then he wrote something at the top of the picture. Before leaving we walked over and read "A pair of elevens out of Coffee Creek, just before the storm."

We took the two fish back down to the boat ramp and released them near the bank of the creek. What a night! What a storm! What a pair of sow bass!

I was thinking, as we ate breakfast the next morning and thoroughly enjoying Juanita's hot biscuits and ranch-grown raw honey. I was also thinking about the Dutch Oven biscuits that Sam Devereaux prepared for us numerous times at an assortment of cookouts and different meals.

I thought it only proper to share his recipe with you. It does take practice to perfect.

DUTCH OVEN BISCUITS

Flour
Salt
Cooking oil
Baking powder
Baking soda

Buttermilk

Place 2 cups twice sifted flour in mixing bowl. Add 2 tablespoons baking powder, $1/_4$ teaspoon baking soda, $1/_3$ teaspoon salt.

Mix dry ingredients thoroughly. Add 1 stick of melted butter. Mix thoroughly so all flour will come in contact with the butter.

Add cold buttermilk, well shaken, and mix with wooden spatula until entire mixture will ball up. Pour ball on floured surface. With sifter, generously cover ball with flour.

Flatten out with palm of hand until mixture is about $3/_4$" thick.

Cut with floured mouth of glass that is $2^1/_2$" to 3" wide. Place cut biscuits in Dutch oven that has bottom covered with cooking oil.

Turn cut biscuits over so that oil will be on both sides.

Bake until golden brown over hot coals.

Place coals on lid so top of biscuits will brown.

These were the kind of biscuits retired Texas Ranger Captain Augustus McCrae made near the beginning of the movie *Lonesome Dove*.

Sam Devereaux was a master with a Dutch Oven, and his biscuits were superb. We called them "cathead" biscuits because when done, they were usually the size of a cat's head or bigger.

This is a story of a world-famous country and western singer that I became friends with. He loved to bass fish and I had the opportunity to run with him for several years. He was nothing in person like he was on the stage.

THE STAR

It was 1978 when The Star and I first crossed paths. Out of a deep respect for our friendship he will be referred to only as "The Star."

He bought a ranch close to my hometown, and we began to occasionally run into each other at a local feed store. He would usually take the time to visit with me for a short period and discuss the Russian Boar in Big Cypress Creek Bottom and how well they were populating the area.

A friend of mine had brought the exotic boar in from South Texas and North Carolina in the last couple of years. It was kind of a novelty project as he spent several thousand dollars propagating the species. His contribution furnished many an outdoorsman with a special treat. Needless to mention, with the inception of the wild boar in the bottoms, the squirrel hunters found new country and more Cypress Bottom squirrels died of old age.

The Star was world-renowned in country music and was recognized as such since I was a youngster. He had turned out hit after hit and most of his albums were number one sellers. He was at the top of the profession and well respected by all his fellow performers. He recently had been selected to perform with the New York Symphony Orchestra.

Even though I was one of his biggest fans and relished the moments with him, we came from different worlds, and the only thing we had in common was our mutual love for wildlife and a deep fondness for running the fast rigs on top of a gentle chop over open water as we pursued the Florida bass, heavy in pre-spawn.

Our first fishing trip happened by chance as we were both unloading at Lake Bob Sandlin early one February morning. We met again and began discussing our individual plans for the day on the water. I mentioned to him that two really big fish had come out of a popular cove the day before and he asked me if I would show him the cove. He followed me down the lake as we headed to the area we had spoken of.

We arrived shortly and with a youthful urgency I shut the big engine off and got on the butt seat with my foot on the trolling motor. He did the same. We moved into a brushy flat area about 8 to 10 feet deep that dropped off into a serpentine creek of approximately 17 feet.

Over the years before impoundment, time had deposited a sand bar of about 3 or 4 feet on the outward bank everywhere the creek bent hard. The cove entered the lake from a northwestern direction and offered some of the warmest water on the lake during the cold months of the year.

Heavy-laden sow bass are attracted to those sandbars, especially if there is brush still on them. Old-timers have told me that reflective rays from the February sun warms those sandy spots and the big bass congregate over the sand because of the warmer temperature. The baitfish begin to leave the deeper channel of the creek as the lake warms up, and they dart over the sandy structures making themselves available sacrifices for the ravenous sows.

That particular day, and I can remember it as if it were yesterday, I had a $^3/_8$ ounce black and blue Stanley jig tied on and a 7-inch black with blue flake Jaw-Tech lizard for my trailer. My friend tied on the exact replica that I pitched him from my tackle box. With him on one side and me on the other we began working the creek bank, from deeper water to shallower.

On his third or fourth throw, he bounced the jig off a large stump and it made a gentle entry into the water. Before the jig had time to hit the bottom, his line began to move away from the stump. As I looked toward him to see his reaction, he was already off the butt seat and standing as he prepared for the hook set. He hit her hard as she rolled and kept moving toward the creek. As she reached the creek, she made a hard pull downward, and I could hear the well-adjusted drag releasing line from the 5500 reel.

My friend was no amateur. He fought with her for a while before bringing her to the surface where she rolled over on her side as my friend slid the mouth of a huge dip net under her. He landed her in magnificent fashion, and I took a photo of him holding a large sow bass that later, at the marina, scaled 11 pounds 3 ounces. He turned to me after placing her in the live well and remarked that she was the biggest bass he had ever caught. He told me that I had brought him luck and we had to start fishing together.

Before that day was over we had boated nine bass with three of them exceeding ten pounds. His first fish was the largest of the day, but he also caught a ten, two nines, and one in the seven-pound range. Our day together had been a fisherman's dream, a day we would never forget.

For the next two weeks, through good weather and bad, we were on a lake every day and caught a boatload of good fish. He caught six more over ten pounds with the largest weighing 12 ½. We fished out of his boat, and I guess I continued to bring him luck or maybe he just wanted me around and said that to make me feel good. Regardless of the reason, the pleasure was all mine.

Our relationship grew, and as we became closer friends through the next seven spawning seasons, he began sharing with me his most harbored feelings and thoughts. No one would ever believe some of the stories he told as he relived his life as a famous country and western musician.

I relished every moment, listening to him illustrate to me what he had done, the places he had been, stories of members of his band, people he had met and performed for, and lastly, the battles he had fought with alcohol and drugs.

We would fish from the middle of February until the last of March each year and then he would be gone on the road or back to Nashville. I would not hear from him except for the distant voice of an occasional call to say hello and relive a past fishing experience.

In his stories, he shared with me the early bouts he had with the booze. He spoke of the nightlife and the honky-tonks. He unloaded on me the mistakes he had made in life, and with seemingly deep regret, he explained to me how he wished he could go back and do it differently. If he could only go back and have an opportunity to set things straight, he could make it right this time.

My friend never intentionally hurt anyone, but many people that he really loved and loved him suffered from his mistakes. Tears sometimes came to his eyes as he spoke of the life he had once lived. He would sometimes refer to it as "wasted years."

As a follower of his, the stories and rumors of the women, the nightlife, and other troubles always trailed him. I heard the stories over and over while growing up, listening to his music. Being with him convinced me that he would never return to those days.

He had recently remarried, this time to a younger woman, who really seemed to care about him. The Star seemed to be truly happy for the first time in many years.

He was clean when I met him, and at no time during the eight years we were together did he ever appear as being under any influence other than the subtle trance brought on from the beauty of nature.

It was March 1987 when we spent our last day together, fishing. He shook my hand and told me that he would see me next season. I helped him load his gear into his Suburban and gave him a big hug.

As I pulled my bass rig out of the parking lot I looked back, and he was waving goodbye to me. Shortly after that my own life took a drastic turn as our family relocated to Texarkana, and I never heard from him again.

Like before we met, I followed his career. He kept producing new hits, and I purchased each one of them and played them over and over as I traveled up and down the highway and, in my office, and at home.

A song of his never played that I did not think of my friend and wondered how he was doing.

A few months after we moved there was a story about him in the newspaper. The article revealed how The Star had been arrested again for possession of cocaine and went on to explain the arrest came just after he had released his latest CD. He had "fallen off the wagon" and upon reading the article, an unexplainable sick feeling settled deep within. Tears came to my eyes and the rest of that day and week he was on my mind.

I did not want to believe the article because I wanted to remember him just as he was when the two of us spent our wonderful days on the water. I want to remember the man I idolized while growing up and later had the privilege of calling a friend.

I am getting in the Jeep and going up into the Kiamichi Mountains tomorrow. I want to ride the country roads around the lakes and the rivers and listen to all of his music that I have recorded on a "stick drive."

When I play those wonderful songs, I will remember only the good times we shared.

.   .   .

As soon as Walter and I finished breakfast, we started making arrangements for the day and tracking the cats to their dens.

We walked down to the barn and loaded our gear and horses on the trailer. Cortez and the Ridgebacks jumped into their box, and we were ready to go. Marjorie had mentioned that she had talked to her neighbor, and we had the green light on wherever we needed to go on his place.

As we pulled out of Marjorie's front entrance, we turned south and traveled about ten miles before entering her neighbor's ranch. After traveling about two miles west, we were near where we had left the cat's trail the previous weekend.

We stopped the truck and began to unload our horses and dogs. It was about 8:30 in the morning, and as soon as we jumped the dogs out, they struck a scent. By the way the dogs acted, it was a strong scent.

The Ridgebacks headed in a direction to the southwest as Cortez trailed along with Walter and me. I had my trusty 270 Winchester, and Walter had a similar rifle in his saddle scabbard.

After about an hour, we made it to the escarpment that we had found the previous week and started the incline that we hoped would lead to where our cats were denned up.

Cortez had become more interested in the trail,

and I knew from past experiences hunting with him that it would not be too long before we saw some action.

The dogs managed to stay out in front of us about 200 yards as they kept their nose to the ground and pushed forward. It was at this time that I noticed a large cat on an isolated ledge about 300 yards from us and several yards above us.

As we moved closer, the cat remained on the ledge as if he was watching the dogs steadily moving in his direction. The dogs got with 100 yards of the cat as he made a move to a higher part of the ledge.

There we stopped, about 230 yards away from him, and I slid the 270 out of the holster and braced myself for a horseback shot from Buck. It was always amazing how Buck would stand tall and firm up when the snap on the saddle holster sounded.

After taking careful aim, the trigger was gently squeezed, and the round sounded as it made its way to the neck area of the mountain lion.

"Great shot," Walter exclaimed. "I didn't know if you could get him from the back of the horse with such ease."

I looked at Walter and replied, "I have taken many

shots similar to the one you just witnessed. Confidence is the secret for success."

When we made it to the downed cat, Cortez had engaged another one nearby, and the fight was on. When we made it to that action, Cortez was standing, chomped down on the neck of a limp cat.

Walter could not believe what he had witnessed, but he did not have time to think very long about it. The Ridgebacks, above us, had sounded, and as we made our way to them, we found that they had another one of the cats denned in its hole.

We could hear the cat hiss and scratch at them as they stuck their noses into the hole for a better smell. After a while, the Ridgebacks began digging a hole beside the den. In about thirty minutes, the cat was exposed, and Cortez had chomped down on his neck.

Walter was really beside himself now after witnessing all of the action and seeing firsthand the dogs do what he had heard me talk of them doing in the past.

We tied the cats off and dragged them back to the truck where we made pictures of all three of them. There were two males and a female. The male weighed about 125 pounds, and the female weighed about 90 pounds.

We called Marjorie and told her of our success. She insisted that we bring the cats to the house so that she could see them.

Upon arrival, we found that Marjorie had called several others who were there to meet us and see the cats.

Walter said, "Marjorie, you have never seen anything like it, the way those dogs worked and overpowered their prey."

"I wish I had been right there with you to see it all," Marjorie said.

Later, one of the visitors remarked that he had seen several of them from a distance but had never seen one up close.

Walter said that years ago there was a "wolfer" that came through occasionally and trapped wolves for a bounty. He remembered him catching a mountain lion one time and wanting a premium bounty for it.

I explained the difficulty in trapping the mountain lions because their sense of smell is so great.

Everyone at Marjorie's was excited, and Juanita remarked to the group, "That will give you all something to talk about for a while."

Walter and the group chuckled as we made plans to dispose of the cats.

My job was finished, the cats were at rest, the baby goats were safe once again, and it was time for me to head north.

Shortly after breakfast the next morning, Cortez, Buck, the Ridgebacks and I pulled out of the main gate and headed to Blanco, Texas. We were headed home.

I GUESS IT IS A LEGACY

To have ever had the opportunity to partake of Marjorie's Hill Country Chocolate Pie, was a once in a lifetime experience for many. I was fortunate to enjoy it regularly as she would prepare it for us when we visited her ranch

MARJORIE BOWLES' HILL COUNTRY CHOCOLATE PECAN PIE

Ingredients:

2 sticks of butter
$5/8$ cup granulated sugar
¾ cup brown sugar packed
½ cup of honey
¼ cup heavy cream
$2/3$ cup chopped bittersweet chocolate, such as El Rey
1 pound of chopped pecans

Make the pie shell or buy ready-made pie dough and follow instructions for baking it until it is ¾ cone.

Preheat oven to 350 degrees. In a saucepan, bring the butter, sugar and honey to a rapid boil. Lower the heat and simmer for 3 minutes until the mixture bubbles.

Add cream, chocolate and pecans and continue to cook and stir until mixture bubbles again. Pour the filling into the prepared pie crust and bake until bubbles appear, about 10 to 12 minutes.

Remove from the oven and chill. Serve cold with coffee ice cream and garnish with a chocolate curl, if desired. Makes a 10 or 12-inch pie.

Pie Crust:

Using your hands, mix 2¾ cups of flour, sifted, with 1 stick of butter and a pinch of salt until the fat is dispersed evenly into small pieces about half the size of a pea. Add 3 tablespoons ice-cold water and knead it just until it comes together. (Overmixing makes a tough crust.) Wrap in plastic and chill for 1 hour.

Preheat oven to 350 degrees. Place chilled dough on a surface that is lightly dusted with flour. Toss a bit of flour on the pie dough and roll out with a rolling pin to ¼ inch thick. Place in a lightly greased-and-flour-dusted pie tin.

Shape dough to the pan and place parchment over the dough; put pie weights (or dried beans or rice) over the paper. Bake until ¾ done. Make sure dough does not get brown. Remove from oven and allow to cool. Remove paper and weights.

.   .   .

Marjorie was my closest Texas Hill Country friend. I loved her and hunted her ranch for 30 years.

Besides the numerous beautiful and precious memories, this pie recipe is all I have left of the many years we spent together.

A jigger or two of good bourbon whiskey can be added to the pie filling if your taste leans that way. Most of the alcohol cooks off and leaves a slight bourbon taste behind.

Good bourbon is all that Marjorie ever served her guests. To this very day, I can close my eyes on a real cold night and still taste the bourbon over the ice cubes and hear the sound of a crackling fire in her big room.

Walter would laugh out, and everyone knew that he was on his way to really enjoying himself; it would not be long before he retired for the evening.

It was always at the time when he started his short giggles that Marjorie would look at me and roll her eyes, insinuating "it will not be long now."

Marjorie bought her whiskey by the gallons in cases from a distributor in San Antonio. She would transfer it to beautiful cut-glass crystal decanters before displaying it and before serving. Her presentation had "class" written all over it.

One Saturday night I was talking about the decanters and how pretty they were. She offered to give me one and even said she would fill it up with her best whiskey if I would accept it.

I turned her down that cold winter night, and many times since then I have wished that I had not.

Cleve was a dear friend that I truly loved. He would have done anything for me that I asked of him. How many people do you know that would do that?

CLEVE

The rains finally came and settled in. There had been one main thing on my mind as I drove into work every day. I watched the weather reports for other parts of the country and had already determined that Stuttgart was getting the same.

The streams and creeks would fill first. The rivers would swell, and the bottoms would flood. The acorns and grain would float, and here would come the ducks. Like always, my gear was packed.

The call came in just before lunch and my secretary forwarded to me. Upon picking up the receiver I heard his distinct voice on the other end.

"Mr. Jim, they are back," was all the caller said.

I thought for a moment...today is Tuesday and maybe with a little shuffling of my schedule I could be there late tomorrow night for an early Thursday hunt.

"Cleve, I will be there tomorrow night," was my reply.

I heard the click on the distant end and knew that my caller had hung up. Cleve was never one to linger and make small talk.

I had met Cleve in 1971 on a Texaco-sponsored duck and goose hunt in the bottoms of Stuttgart, Ark. My group hunted three days, and Cleve had been assigned to us as a guide.

His responsibilities and duties were to make sure that upon arrival, we were properly checked into the lodge, transport us to and from the field, make sure the blinds were ready, decoys set properly, food and refreshment packed in the gear, and to serve as dog handler.

In the lodge at night, around the glowing fire, we would discuss how good Cleve was at his job. Often the discussion led to how Cleve could work for any of us in our respective businesses and what an asset he would be to the company.

Cleve had grown up nearby to the lodges at Stuttgart and had started working there as a young boy, splitting firewood. Through his teen years he had been called upon to accept more and more responsibility.

He cared for the brood females and assisted in

caring for their puppies. Each season three females were bred to keep the retriever line alive. That retriever line dated back to colonial times and would not be allowed to die out. Each year, pups were selected to continue the lineage and the rest were sold to outside interests. There was a waiting list to get on the list for one of those quality pups.

Cleve was taught dog grooming and retriever training. Unlike most of the other handlers, he had a gentle way when it came to teaching them to retrieve.

Retrievers are born with an instinct to pick up and "fetch" an object. Most successful handlers force break their charges to retrieve. Force breaking to retrieve can be a painful experience for some dogs, especially if they have a bit of a stubborn streak in them.

Force breaking could be used on dogs of all ages, and the older they were the more stubbornness they generally displayed. Some force breakers delight in showing off their dog's skill by having them retrieve anything on command. I once saw a handler command a dog to pick up a rock and carry it back to the truck. This saddened me, and I never thought the same of the guide after that.

Cleve did not believe in force breaking and had his own way of getting the job done. Firmness, repetition, kindness and reward worked best for him.

He used the table, just as the force breakers did, but his method with the table allowed him to keep his hands close to, and almost in constant contact with, his young pupils.

Cleve did not hunt a dog that was not finished, and I never saw one of his dogs refuse to go and get a duck or goose. Cleve never raised his voice at his dogs and would move their positions in the field with a soft whistle and a wave of the arm.

Through the years, Cleve and I became close friends, and I would always remember him on each visit by bringing along something I thought he would use.

It had to be useable or Cleve did not care much for it. I learned this after several years of bringing him different items. Lanyards for whistles and calls were probably his favorite, even though he never admitted it.

New fancy duck calls seemed to be his least favorite. He would keep them in a glass covered case in his cabin. He would always thank me, but I never saw him blow one and I definitely didn't see him use one. After a few trips with duck calls, I got the message.

Not that he did not use a call, but the calls he used

were the ones he had made. I asked him one time about his handmade calls, and he told me he preferred the sounds that he could make with them. He explained that when the bottoms were flooded the calls took on different sounds, "black magic sounds" as he would like to refer to them.

And my friend could serenade the ducks and geese with his black magic sounds. He had very few "fly-bys," and the ones that did would usually bank, return, and hit the "blocks." It was almost impossible for them to stay away.

He drank Old Crow bourbon whiskey and smoked King Edward cigars and very seldom had to buy either. His clients saw that his supply of both was well stocked.

He kept a plug of Day's Work in a pocket of his bib overalls and an old Kabar knife in another. He wore knee-high rubber boots and a John Deere cap year around.

I asked him one time if he would use a new shotgun if we were to bring him one. He said he would, and he would like for it to be a Remington pump.

When I got back to the office I ordered him a new Remington 870. I asked the dealer to engrave Cleve over the ejection chamber. Two of my hunting buddies split the cost with me, and we planned to give it to him on our next trip.

That trip came on New Year's Eve in 1979 and like so many years since then, the New Year's duck and goose hunt had become a tradition for us.

We left out early that morning and my Chevy Suburban was loaded with hunters and their gear. We were all excited about the four days off and returning to what we all loved to do.

Duck hunting was to us what cocaine must be to the user. Sitting in the dark blind, waiting on the first flight is a natural high which I have always had difficulty replicating.

Cleve met us at the lodge, and after we unloaded our gear we all sat down in the living room in front of a blazing fire. Scotch was the preferred evening drink, and we did indulge. The temperature outside was 22 and falling. We had watched it on the automobile since we had left home, and it steadily fell the entire trip.

Cleve mixed drinks, and after a while we broke out the new shotgun and made a formal presentation to our friend. He showed excitement that I had never witnessed from him before. He picked it up, lifted it to his shoulder and swung it away from us.

He lowered it and saw "Cleve" engraved over the ejection chamber. When he looked up I could see tears in his eyes. The observation made me want to cry with him.

Such experiences last a lifetime in your memories, and I do not dare to try and count the many times I have thought about that presentation since then.

As usual, Cleve had us a big dinner prepared, and after the scotch had captured our minds, we sat down to eat. The chicken-fried steak, gravy, mashed potatoes, green beans, made-from-scratch rolls, and the tossed green salad were excellent. The fire was inviting and the fiddle music after dinner was not bad.

Cleve said "goodnight" about 9:30, and we turned in. Cleve told us that he would return about midnight and stoke the fire. He would return again about 4:30 to make sure we were awake and to have coffee and breakfast with us. It was always my job to prepare the first morning's breakfast, and Cleve had everything that I needed in the refrigerator.

After breakfast, we had another cup and started getting dressed for the adventure that awaited us; that cold adventure, on the water, shooting ducks.

The outside thermometer showed it had warmed up during the night and read 28 degrees. The wind was gentle out of the north and that meant that passing shots could be expected, especially if the

wind picked up.

Our blind was positioned backed up to some tall reeds to the north. The blocks were placed in a wide intermittent "vee," south of our concealment. That would put the ducks landing in front of us, into the wind. They were more vulnerable with wings cupped.

Cleve had an old Chevy van that he transported his crew from the lodge to the field. There was ample room for all of us, our gear, and the two dogs. We loaded up in the van and headed down a semi-frozen road which, as Cleve explained, was so muddy the day before that it was barely passable.

There was a sense of descending into the bottoms, and in about 30 minutes we were in walking distance of our blind. It was a large blind, heavily caned, and built just the way that Cleve had always built his blinds in the past. It was half-mooned with a bench in the back with comfortable chairs mounted to it. There were two kerosene heaters to keep the chill away and flats built on each end on the front of the blind that served as pedestals for the dogs to stand sentry.

Cleve pointed out the two entrances from the rear, and we all entered and took our positions. Hot coffee from the thermoses and a touch of apricot brandy sure warmed the twenty-minute wait before first flight and legal shooting time.

The wait passed quickly as I heard Cleve say, "first flight," with his head down and his finger pointed up.

I looked at my watch, and we still had a couple of minutes before we could start the hunt. When I looked up I heard the swoosh of air through their wings, as they flew over us into the wind, with wings cupped and hit the open "vee" in the blocks.

Northern mallards, 12 drakes and 10 hens, scattered and started feeding. It was amazing to witness how still the dogs were with the flock so close to us. Their eyes were the only moving parts as they kept a constant vigil on the feeding waterfowl.

Cleve said, "It is time, and we will take the next bunch that comes in."

And come they did. Over and over again ... until we all had our limits. Cleve handled the dogs perfectly, and they were a beauty to watch as they retrieved each bird and returned it to their master's hand.

Mallards, Gadwalls, Shovelers, Pintails, Snows and four Canvasback drakes. There were several Wood Ducks that came in, but we never shot them. They are the only ones that do not migrate and stay around year after year, and besides, they are too pretty to kill.

The afternoon hunt was great also. One hunter in our group took several pictures of the ducks hitting the "vee." We mostly just sat in the blind, sampled a sip or two of that apricot brandy and watched the ducks work the decoys as Cleve serenaded them with his "black magic calls."

Roasted duck with all the trimmings was the main menu for the night, and Cleve brought in his niece, Susie, to prepare the meal for us. The fire roared, the wind outside howled, and we enjoyed our cocktails before dinner.

Cleve cleaned the rest of the day's hunt and vacuum sealed them for the freezer. My group would always take frozen duck home to wives that very seldom wanted to cook them. In my later years I realized that the ducks were evidence they had really gone with me to hunt.

Cleve fed the dogs and returned them to their kennel. He came back in and washed his hands, sat down in an old rope rocker in front of the fire, while I prepared for him a taste of the "Old Bird."

He liked it straight with two cubes of ice. By the second swallow, the ice was all gone, and he wiped his mouth with the back of his hand and exclaimed, "There is nothing like Old Crow on a cold afternoon after a good day of duck hunting." We stoked the fire, and Susie announced it was dinner time.

After that the lodge got pretty quiet for a while as we devoured her wonderful cooking. Our wives would not have believed it if they had wanted to...how good the meal was.

Three more days of the same, and we were out of there. Upon leaving, we all told Cleve "goodbye," until next time, and tipped him well for his efforts.

I asked him if he would enjoy a quail hunt to West Texas in the fall. This would give him an opportunity to check out his wing shot with his new 870. He said he would, and I told him I would set it up and give him a call and directions to my house.

.   .   .

October brought promise of a bountiful quail season on the lease in West Texas. The rains had come at the right time and the birds and the feed were plentiful. There was adequate "broom weed" coverage, and the baby birds we had observed earlier in the summer had flourished and done well.

I gave Cleve a call and set up the hunt with him. It

was planned for the third weekend. We all checked our gear and cleaned our shotguns. New O-rings were put in the 1100s and springs finely lubricated in the Brownings.

Cleve arrived at my house on Thursday afternoon in his old Chevy truck with an aluminum dog box in the back. I met him in the yard and gave him a big hug and handshake.

I told Cleve that we had the dogs and asked him why he brought the dog box. He motioned for me to follow him to the rear of the truck.

"Mister Jim, I brought you a surprise," was his only reply. He opened the tailgate and the dog box and out stepped a beautiful Chesapeake female.

Cleve said her name was "Julie," and she was mine. I cupped her head in my hands and looked deep into her beautiful green eyes for some time.

When I looked up at Cleve he was looking right at me with tears in his eyes. At that time, I felt the tears come to my eyes as I hugged Cleve again and told him how much I appreciated the gesture.

"She is fully trained," he said, as he closed the door on the dog house. I put her on a leash, and we walked her to my kennel. I told Cleve that I really hated to leave her behind while we were gone.

He told me to pet her good and feed her and she would be fine until we returned. I filled her automatic feeder and cleaned her waterer. As I closed the kennel gate behind us, I thought how lucky a man I was to have such a friend.

Julie was from the old lineage, and Cleve had made arrangements for her when she was six weeks old. She was to be mine when he had finished her. She was in the kennel in Stuttgart when we were there, but Cleve never mentioned having her in his care.

Today, as I sit and think about those days, tears come to my eyes once more. Cleve is gone and most of my hunting buddies, like myself, are in our twilight years. We still get together occasionally, and when we do, the brandy flows freely, and the memories run rampant.

And yes, we do talk about how much we miss Cleve.

MELBA RAY SOONER

Thought of Melba Ray Sooner this morning when I was thumbing through my field notes from pheasant hunts in the Texas Panhandle. Ran across this delicious recipe that she prepared for us many years ago and was nice enough to give me a copy for my collection.

If you ever make it one time, you will make it again; it was that good.

CARAMEL APPLE DUMP CAKE

An easy to make, delicious cake that has only four ingredients. Serve with whipped cream or ice cream.

Cook time: 50 minutes; Prep time 10 minutes; Serves: 12

Ingredients:

2 cans (21 ounces) apple pie filling
1 box (16 ounces) butter golden or spice cake mix
1 cup butter, melted
$1/2$ cup caramel sauce, like you, would put on ice cream
$1/2$ teaspoon cinnamon
1 cup chopped pecans

Directions:

1. In a greased 9 X 13-inch baking dish, mix apple pie filling and caramel sauce. Add cinnamon. Spread evenly in the pan.

2. Pour dry cake mix directly on top of the pie filling and spread evenly.

3. Top with melted butter and pecans.

Bake at 350 degrees for 50-55 minutes or until the top is golden brown and apple filling is bubbly.

FIRE ANTS

One spring we had an abundance of rain, and there were fire ants everywhere: They were definitely on the move, establishing new colonies.

Walter shared his personal fire ant killer formula with me: the orange oil recipe for killing fire ants. This instantly kills them. He used 2 oz. orange oil, 2 oz. blue Dawn dish soap to 1 gallon of water. Spraying or pouring a small portion of this mixture directly on the fire ant mound and around it will work. In about three days, they will be gone, and there will be no activity at that site.

MOSQUITO REPELLENT

Back by popular demand from last summer! This got rave reviews including places in the world where the mosquitoes are the worst!

For those of you with mosquito invasions. Here's an easy and pleasant repellent recipe you can make at home:

Combine in a 16 oz. bottle:
15 drops lavender oil
3-4 tablespoons of vanilla extract

$1/4$ cup lemon juice
Fill bottle with water.
Shake and ready to use as a topical spray.

Make some extras to gift to your neighbors, family and friends. Trust me, it'll be appreciated!

A WONDERFUL HUNT IN THE TURKEY PENS

January found my circle of quail hunters with an invite to come and hunt the turkey pens in Clifton, Texas. Gosh, what a memorable and productive hunt it was.

Many will not believe what we witnessed and the amount of quail that we harvested from the pens that were covered with weed seed after the domestic turkeys were gathered, processed and sold by Lacy Feed Company.

All these years later, this three-day hunt invariably stands out in my mind as one of the finest conditions that we ever followed the dogs.

Everything was ideal, and the pointers worked perfectly each day in finding and setting the coveys. Singles were so numerous that many were walked up as we hurriedly moved to the next covey point. Hunting sacks filled with the upland game bird were taken as we moved along inside the pens.

All the turkeys that had inhabited the pens had been removed prior to the Thanksgiving and Christmas holidays. The wonderful climate had allowed the weed seeds to germinate and grow to a height of approximately three feet; thus, the perfect bird cover. There was an abundance of feed and hiding places for the game we hunted.

Three Hispanic guides busied themselves with taking quail back to the trucks and bringing additional shells for us to continue our hunt. This continued for three days.

I will not even attempt to express how many birds we took from the feed pens; all I can tell you—it was unbelievable.

Today, even after the many years, I get excited reliving the adventure and putting it on paper for my readers. You just would have had to have been there by my side and witnessed it along with me to believe it like it happened.

There was twelve-foot tall chicken wire, the kind with the octagon form of holes in it. It was held in place by metal posts, and the wire was attached with wire clips. Each pasture or pen contained anywhere from 35 to 75 acres, and sometimes we would have to walk for quite a distance to get to the point where a gate had been constructed in the fence. That was the only way to pass from one pen to another.

It was right after the noon hour on the second day of hunting when the dogs made rock solid points on a tank dam that was near a corner of one of the pens. Quail started getting up, one covey after another, with as many as 100 quail to each covey. Many of them winged and banked back toward the tall fence, and when they did, it left almost a full covey stuck that flew into the wire.

As we placed the birds in our hunting sacks, one friend remarked, "I wonder what they will say when it is discovered that none of these fence birds have any shot in them?"

That remark brought chuckles from the group as we continued to pull the birds out of the wire. Gosh, it was quite a hunt.

It was the coldest part of January as the winter sun lowered in the southwest, we loaded the dogs back in their warm cargo boxes that were filled with warm hay. They would be fed back at the hotel before we called it a night.

That would be a while because we had hundreds of birds to clean before we showered and cleaned up for dinner.

It was the end of the second day afield, and on our way back to Waco, we stopped on the banks of the Brazos River and cleaned 100 birds from the day's efforts by the headlights of the trucks. What a cold job it was. The balance of our harvest was left with our Hispanic helpers that processed them and placed them on ice for us to pick up the next day.

As the last few of the quail we dressed beside the Brazos River were pitched on ice, W. L. Weller was ushered in, and after that the night only got better.

The 100 dressed birds went to new friends of ours that we had made during the previous nights at the Melody Ranch. Our last night in town we were surprised with a wonderful fried quail dinner with all the trimmings. There is nothing like good friends on the road.

We arrived back at our motel in Waco, fed our dogs, showered and cleaned up, and as we sat around the fire pit in the courtyard, we reminisced about the day and most of the shots taken with their result. W. L. dealt us a "pat" hand, and as we finished off his quart offerings, another one was broken out.

After our hot showers, we had dinner that evening next door at the Longhorn Steakhouse. When we finished a delicious meal, we retired to the motel.

There are few things as nice as a hot shower after a long, cold day hunting in the turkey pens.

Toasts ran rampant way into the night, and before we knew it, we were in the wee hours of morning with another day left of our adventure. We had to get to bed if we were going to get any sleep before our last day's hunt.

Deep sleep came fast because we all were exhausted from our day, and W. L. did not have to do much rocking before we were all out.

I guess that was one of the shortest nights of my life, and when the alarm did sound at five thirty, we were up and at it, preparing for our last day on the turkey ranges.

After a big breakfast in Clifton, Texas, and meeting up with our local hunters, we made our way back to the turkey pens.

It was almost seven-thirty when we jumped the dogs out of their boxes and allowed them time to run and clean out.

They were fed dry dog food, and as they ate, we prepared for the day's hunt by loading our shell bags. Each of us got into our hunting clothes and situated them to our own personal liking.

A high-energy dry dog food was always fed before starting a day in the field. Canned or moist dog food always seemed to affect the dog's smelling ability for the first couple of hours of the hunt.

This last day was no different than the other two. We got into the game almost as soon as we left the trucks. From there, it only got better.

We followed the dogs and gunned every covey point; many times, we just let the singles go. The only time they were shot was when we accidentally stepped near one in the thick cover as we were making our way to the next point and the single got up on its own.

Quail are not migratory, and we were allowed to hunt them with five shot load capacity shotguns.

It was not unusual for one of us to down as many as seven on a covey rise before we had to reload. I was very fortunate one time and brought down nine. No, it was not as easy as pulling them out of the chicken wire, but it did not take long to get a hunting sack full together.

That day's hunt was near comparable to only a half dozen other days in my career afield. All I can say now is, "Wow, unbelievable," and I pause, take a deep breath, and ask myself, "Where did I get the energy to do it all?"

As an old man, it tires me now just mentally reliving the excitement. It all left such an indelible mark on my being.

After the third day, near dark, we all said goodbye to Lacy Feed Company and the overgrown turkey pens that offered us such superb quail hunting. It was sad when we left, like saying "bye" to an old friend who you might not see again.

The experience had an unexplainable effect on me. For the next couple of weeks, I more or less went through withdrawal symptoms from leaving the turkey pens. It was near the end of my really hard pursuit of the upland game bird and maybe I was transgressing that move.

Whatever the reasons, they were of my own volition; I found no reason of having to explain them. It was only more grist to personally mill in my mind when the days would come that I was not able to go afield as I once did.

The reels in my mind are full now; I knew such days were coming.

I have often thought hard about how much I loved it and have taken the time to momentarily ask myself, "If given the chance to go back as a young man, would you do it all over again?"

After careful deliberation, and very little hesitation, I tell myself that certainly, knowing what I know now, I would do it all over again.

As often prompted from my closest friends, I am the first to understand that I might just be trying to fool myself.

THE MESCALERO APACHES

The Mescalero Apaches developed originally from Asia and from nomadic hunters and gatherers that eventually settled in and roamed the Southwest. They were experts in guerrilla warfare and were highly skilled horsemen after the horse came to their lands.

Apache women were known for their ability to find and prepare food from many different plant sources.

The people of the Southwest were given the name "Mescalero" because they gathered and ate the mescal plant. It was the staple of their diets and could sustain them in both good times and bad.

Harold Waters, (High Eagle), was a full blood Apache and was a friend of mine. We had met at a national young farmer's convention in Phoenix, Arizona back in the late 1970s. We immediately were attracted to each other, and over the years our friendship only grew.

I was working a New Holland farm equipment booth during the convention, and Harold's dairy products booth was two booths down from me.

Harold came to Northeast Texas several times and fished with me. He met me in West Texas on the bird leases at least a half dozen times.

I went on my first bear hunt with him and some of his kinfolks on the "rez" (Apache Reservation) in New Mexico. Around their fires, I first experienced eating bear meat and the way they prepared it made it delectable.

Bear meat contains more fat than beef, and the meat tastes very rich and sometimes leaves a hint of sweetness on your palate.

One late fall, Harold asked me to bring my dogs and try and silence some of the mountain lions that were killing their calves, sheep and young goats.

I loaded my gear, my horse and mule, Cortez and the Ridgebacks, extra feed and water for all of us, replenished the chuck box, and we hit the road headed West.

It was almost 25 hours of highway before we finally arrived where we were going. I took a five-hour layover in El Paso for a nap before heading out again.

Upon arrival, Harold and his friends were awaiting us, and after several hours of catching up on what each of us had been doing since we last talked, we drove on up and pitched a base camp in the foothills of the Gila Mountains.

The camp would be our home for the next few days as we attempted to rid the land of the pesky varmints.

The dogs and I had taken many mountain lions out of the Kiamichi Mountains of Southeastern

Oklahoma and panthers out of Lake Fork as it was filling with water, but I had never attempted cats the size of the ones in western New Mexico. We were in for a real surprise.

On earlier bear hunts, I had observed the mountain lions of that country from a distance, and when the glass was placed on them, it could easily be determined that they were larger and heavier.

Finding their tracks in soft ground substantiated that they were many pounds heavier; the tracks were deeper.

It was late one afternoon on such a previous hunt that I discovered a mountain lion trailing our party. He was on a ledge behind us and at a higher elevation. It is not uncommon for a mountain lion to strike a scent on humans and begin trailing it.

I have read where hunters in Mexico had been attacked by mountain lions that were trailing them. On that particular afternoon, when we did notice the big cat surveying his prey, we immediately stopped and set up camp for the night. We knew that there was a good chance of getting a shot at him while he observed us making camp.

That afternoon, we had a Marine Corp sniper in our hunting party, and by the time the coffee was brewing, he had strategically placed a high powered 270 Winchester slug through the chest of our unwanted visitor. We all stood and watched as the big cat tumbled from the ledge it was on.

We dragged the cat in by horseback and estimated his weight at 180-190 pounds. His feet were as large as a pie plate.

That was about twice the size of the cats that Cortez and I had had experiences with. We were in for a definite surprise this time.

As we bedded down for the night, I drifted off to sleep thinking about an earlier book in which Cleve and his Indian friend had killed a huge mountain lion not too far from this camp, in the Gila Mountains. It is amazing how some things, if allowed enough time, will come full circle.

That was such a peaceful sleep with the temperature falling about 15 degrees after the sun totally set. Those extra blankets I had brought and unrolled before turning in really felt good.

The next morning was ushered in with Harold filling a huge metal coffee pot and placing it over hot coals from a fire that he had already started.

I arose and pulled my jeans and boots on and dragged up a big limb from a nearby log to sit on. Harold's brother, Doug, poured us a cup, and our day was officially started.

The sun was beginning to peep over the eastern mountainous horizon as we had our second cup and the rest of the group joined in on our conversations.

Six of us scarfed down a delicious breakfast of eggs, biscuits, gravy, bacon and a slab of ham; food is always at its best under such conditions and surroundings, and with certain friends.

Canteens were filled from the water tanks, and the horses were fed and watered. After that, we saddled the horses and packed the mules for the day's adventure in the hills.

I had gotten up about an hour before everyone else and had already fed and watered Cortez and the Ridgebacks. I had brought all six of them. Their eagerness for a new trail over new country was very evident.

I had my faithful gelding, Buck, and a strong little shining black mule I called "Slick." They were standing near the trailer with their gear on.

Buck was saddled, and Slick was carrying a pack rack that already had the gear loaded. I had developed a neat trick of packing a sack and attaching it to the pack rack without much effort.

It would ride comfortably all day over rough terrain and never offer any problems of coming loose or falling off. Across the pack rack and on top rode my second saddle holster that carried the Weatherby 300 Magnum. It was scoped to the hilt and was only pulled for a long serious shot.

The scoped Winchester 270 was cased in my holster on Buck, and under my left arm was a Smith and Wesson Model 29 - $8^3/_8$-inch 44 Magnum. It was open sighted and rode in a front break-away leather clasped shoulder holster.

All three firearms had proven themselves many times over, and I relied on them for my firepower when hunting and tracking.

The rest of the hunters in my group were similarly equipped.

As the morning sun peeped over the eastern horizon, it was time for us to unchain the dogs and swing up into our saddles.
With the dogs scampering and enjoying their new-found freedom and with our pack mules following us, we hit the trail headed north around the eastern side of a large mountain.

Our goal was to reach Six Mile Boulders by midday. Six Mile Boulders were a large exhibition of exposed rock that pushed themselves out of the side of a mountain possibly during the time the earth was being formed. They were quite a landmark and were interesting to view and talk about during a break from the trail.

They also, in the past, had offered shelter to us from a storm or cold wind. Yes, we had been that way before, and the Indian hunters with me had been there many times.

It was impossible to grow up around the Gila Mountains and not know where Six Mile Boulders were located.

It was a little past noon when we made it to our destination for the morning. There was a clear stream flowing out of the mountains from above, and all of us took our portion from it. The horses, the mules and the dogs also drank from the clean mountain stream. Its pristine condition was mentioned and compared to what it must have been like down through time, offering many a drink of water for sojourners on the mountain paths.

The conditions were so ideal at Six Mile Boulders, we decided to make camp and spend the rest of the afternoon and night beside the free-flowing stream. I could not help but think of the Coor's advertisement of "brewed with clear mountain water" when I looked at the babbling stream.

The water from the stream did make some of the best coffee I ever had. My whole group acknowledged that as we partook of its unique taste.

The temperature was colder as night approached, and we had only moved north a few miles. Our gain in elevation was significant because the farther we went, the slower we got.

As gravity increased on the trail, we would all tire easier, and the horses and mules would show the fatigue first.

Our ending destination was a small summer Apache village about another day's ride from Six Mile Boulders.

There, Harold's kinfolks spent their summers and retreated back to the flat land on the reservation during the cooler part of the year. It was from that camp that Harold was notified that mountain lions were playing havoc with their young calves and goats.

My mission was to bring my dogs, my horse and mule, and other gear to join the mountainous hunt. Everyone involved knew that there was not going to be anything easy about tracking and destroying our prey.

Once I received the call, it took me one full day to get all my stuff loaded and prepared for the long trip and hunting excursion.

Close friends of mine back home warned me, because of the size of our prey, they thought I was possibly biting off more than I could chew in pursuing the Arizona mountain lions. We had never hunted a creature of this size and prowess; our work was definitely cut out for us. I had earlier decided that the dogs and I were ready to accept the challenge.

Once that decision was made, there was no turning back on our end; we were rolling West.

Cortez was in his sixth year, and the four Ridgebacks were aged three to five years. Basically, they were all in the prime of their life and had many hours of tracking and finding what we were hunting. They were extremely experienced in knowing how to handle our prey once we closed in. Together, they had never been defeated; there were no plans of anything different happening this time.

The trail from Six Mile Boulders on up to the small Apache village they called Tope, was treacherous to travel. On the trail, I asked myself several times why I did not bring my big riding mule, Rue, instead of Buck.

We labored on, and within about five more slow and careful hours, we arrived at Tope.

I was surprised to find about 15 of the tribe members that inhabited the village through the summer months.

The nights were getting much cooler, and the Apaches were in the process of preparing to return to the flat land. They wanted to stay to see what kind of success we had with the mountain lions that had been killing their stock.

We were received well by the villagers, and the food that we brought on the trail was of much higher quality that what they were eating. They were happy to sit around our fires and share our food. Harold interpreted much of the conversation from the villagers.

As the campfires died down the first night, I had a good feeling about the mission we were on. Our success would make a lot of difference with these people; our efforts could be well rewarded.

Shortly after a hearty breakfast for all and about an hour after the sun peeped over the horizon, we were saddled and riding the trail to where the animals had been taken.

Upon arriving at a small mountain pasture and talking to the lone Apache guard that had been sitting with the herd of livestock, we determined that we would halt at a makeshift camp and allow the dogs to hunt the surroundings. They could possible pick up a good scent, or maybe we could cut a track on one of the critters we sought.

By mid-morning, we had a strike. One of the Ridgebacks had struck a scent about a half of a mile from our makeshift camp and had sounded. The rider with her mentally marked the spot and rode in to give us a report.

Once the trail was determined, our real hunt was on.

Past experiences had proven that the trails usually led higher into the mountains. After a few minutes on the trail that we had found, that theory proved itself again; the mountain lion associated safety with height in a mountain hideout.

As we moved forward, the trail became more rigorous.

The dogs were on the scent, and it was noticeable that their smell was becoming stronger.

The anticipation of what awaits us at the end of the trail adds to our excitement as hunters. It is that excitement that pushes us on and beckons us to succeed in our endeavors.

Just before the sun sank behind the western mountain terrain, the trail split. That meant that there were at least two cats we were tracking.

That thought was substantiated when we reached soft dirt and could easily distinguish we had more cats than just one.

We stopped and unsaddled our mounts as we started putting our gear away for the night. I took the cross buck from Slick and propped it up on one side to make for a place to lean to and rest my back as we sat around the fire. It was quite comfortable after I threw the two saddle blankets over it.

This location was a perfect place to quit the trail for the day and pitch camp for the night. There was fresh mountain water nearby, and it was not long before fires were going, and our evening meal was cooking. A large pot of coffee was brewing, and the cast iron skillets were hot.

Skillet-braised antelope steak that we had taken on the trail, and fried skillet Irish potatoes complemented the meal; it was thoroughly enjoyed by all.

When I crawled into my bedroll, it did not take me long to drift off in a deep sleep. Cool, fresh mountain air causes that with me every time.

As I drifted away, my thoughts returned to Cleve Welling and his Indian friend, the little brother of Geronimo, and how, back in the mid-1800s, they had taken the monstrous mountain lion not too far from where we were now. My excitement was growing.

There would be nothing more delightful than to also take a huge mountain lion out of the Gila Mountain Range. Gosh, I wrote about it, and now I am living it firsthand. How rewarding; how thankful I am for the opportunity.

The next few days could become very exciting for me and my group of native hunters.

Dogs become restless when they are pulled from a hot trail for any reason and especially for a night's rest. They never comprehend why we must stop and sleep in preparation for continuing the hunt the next day.

In their minds, it is only natural to think that once a trail has been struck, it is only over when the prey is killed, caught or run down. They will never understand this stopping to rest for the night.

This time was no different, and every time I woke during the night, the dogs were up on their feet, watching me, and ready to resume the trail. Good hunting dogs are just not programmed for this kind of a chase.

Morning finally came and as soon as it was light enough to travel the treacherous trail before us and we had finished our breakfast, we broke camp and left out. The excitement was in the air, and it was very noticeable that the intensity level was increasing for all of us.

AN EARLIER BEAR HUNT

I was thinking, it was exactly four years ago last month that I was with the same group and on the same trail, black bear hunting in the Gila Mountains.

Harold, his two brothers and cousins had invited me and a friend from Idalou, Texas, for a big bear hunt just before hibernation time. That is when the bears are their fattest and carrying extra weight for their winter sleep.

A bear taken at this time was proclaimed a delicacy by those that appreciate the meat. Their meat is dark, rich, and has a hint of sweetness to it. The bear steaks cut from the hind quarters can be grilled into delectable pieces that can top off any meal.

We selectively took three mid-size bears on that particular hunt and feasted on bear meat for several days as we sought out our prey.

Bear meat is excellent to make jerky when you finally dry most of the fat out of it.

Cortez was only two back then, but he had already proven himself as an outstanding tracker, hunter and fighter.

The female Ridgebacks were about the same age and together with Cortez they made formidable opponents for almost anything in the mountains.

Rue was with me on that trip, and I used Slick to carry the pack rack and tote our gear along. I hauled both of them and the dogs all the way from Northeast Texas and the trip was as long then as it is now.

At night, the temperatures would fall, and it made a good fire and a blanket feel just right. The mescal that my friends had made only complemented the surroundings and allowed everything to come together at the right time.

The second night on the trial, my friends broke out the peace pipe and the mixture that we puffed was quite strong. It noticeably made me light headed when I attempted to stand up.

They never told me the ingredients even though I asked them several times. It had to be some kind of dope, and they knew if they told me I would not smoke it.

Dope is one thing that, fortunately, I was able to stay away from my entire life. I had friends who used it and quite frequently. I observed firsthand the damage it can do to an individual.

I could write a complete book on how dope has messed up the lives of many that I have known and how it has completely destroyed some others.

My reply to them when asked to join them was, "I get crazy enough with what runs out of the bottle, thank you. I have never needed anything more."

The peace pipe initially left a burn in the mouth and throat but after the second or third pass around it became smoother.

Harold laughed and remarked that his father may have been on the pipe when he gave him the name, High Eagle. Harold was the first to admit that enough of the smoke would definitely make a person "high" and could cause hallucinations.

I experienced some really wild dreams that night wrapped up in a sleeping bag in front of the fire. I started off cold and woke up coming out of the bag. I would doze back off, and there was something chasing me down a narrow mountain trail.

Once, during my wild dreams, I saw a huge bear standing and offering me a pipe filled with what looked like the same concoction that had me wound up.

The strange thing about all of this is the dreams did not come back to me until two or three days later. Then they appeared as clear as if they had really happened. I could never explain that lapse of time.

I told Harold about the dreams as they came to me later. He only laughed and said, "Jim, you must spend some time with us in the sweat lodges."

"If the sweat lodges are anything like what I experienced, I do not want any part of them," I replied.

A couple of years later, I did go to the sweat lodge with my friends, but when the pipe was passed, I declined.

After the bout with the pipe, I was more or less unsure about continuing the trail the next morning. Even during saddling up and preparation for the day, I still felt a little "woozy."

After breakfast, the sensation began to leave me. After about mid-morning, I was okay again. I can remember that feeling until this day.

It was almost noon when the dogs struck the trail of what we presumed to be a bear. We followed the dogs for a couple of hours, and when we caught up with them, they had "bayed" at a large opening in the side of the mountain. It possible could be an entrance to a cave.

There were tracks everywhere, but they were not bear tracks; they were huge cat tracks.

After thoroughly discussing what we had found, we pulled the dogs off and returned to our camp that we had occupied the night before. We had decided we were after bear, and we did not want to hunt mountain lions on this trip.

This was one of the determining factors of why we were here now, hunting mountain lions. We had seen some giant tracks and wanted to find what was making them.

Personally, I wanted one of those big cats that Cleve Welling and his Indian friend had killed back in the 1850s, the one that I wrote about in *Trail Justice, the Jess Logan Saga*.

Regardless of the reasons, it had taken the biggest part of four years for us all to hook back up again and fulfill that dream. Now, we were living it.

The bear hunt lasted for five days, and it was a total success. There were no problems on the trail, and the dogs and stock were very manageable; very few times is that the case.

We took three nice bears and dined on some real fine meals, as we continued our hunt. Harold's little brother saved the claws and made me a claw necklace for a souvenir of the trip and to bring me luck in my life's journey. That necklace still hangs today in my office and occasionally I take it down for a closer look.

When I do, the memories run rampant, and I am instantly drawn back to the mountains, to the friendships and the camaraderie of the particular outing. Minutes become moments as the sand falls through the hourglass in my mind; the magic of the claws is still there.

After five days in the hills, we returned to their homes on the flat lands. The next day, I loaded all my animals, bid my friends farewell, and headed the Dodge and gooseneck back east. A long trip was before us.

As I finally got onto the interstate, the distance did not seem to bother me much; it allowed me plenty of time to think about the previous five days with friends.

Later, that time in the mountains with friends would become as a dream, dreamed high in the Gila Mountains by a warm fire on a cold night; a wonderful dream to drift off to sleep with; such comforting thoughts remain until this day.

I have used that setting more than once to drift off to sleep. They were such pleasant memories.

BACK TO THE BIG CATS

We had been moving north about 30 minutes when Cortez pulled the scent off the breeze. He stood tall, and you could sense that he was working with a familiar smell that he had known in the past.

About the same time, the Ridgebacks pulled the same scent, and all of them became alert and mustered to the center of the trail ahead of us.

I knew that things could get serious and it would be a good idea to check weapons and other gear that had us engaged on this mission. There were too many high ridges in close proximity of where our party was traversing.

I unbuckled the fancy snap on the saddle holster and made the Winchester 270 more readily available in case it was needed. My eyes constantly scanned the ridges for any type of movement along our way.

Buck, from years of experience, steadied when he heard the snap unbutton. I nudged him forward with the toe of my boots and told him, "Not yet, old friend."

Mountain lions are quiet and stalking; whereas, the panthers will scream and let you know that they are near. The two creatures are completely different in those ways.

The mountain lion like the vantage point of height so they can observe your actions, many times while remaining hidden from view. The dogs and I had much experience hunting big cats south of the border in Old Mexico. We had engaged them several times over the years and had learned much about the larger cats' behavior.

Until then, our only experience with mountain lions had come from the ones we brought out of the Kiamichi Mountains of South East Oklahoma. These cats were much smaller with the largest male going almost 100 pounds. Females weighed in around 75-80 pounds.

The individuals that we sought on this trip, these Gila Mountain cats, were almost twice that in size and weight.

About that time, we came to a wider spot in our trail and the nearby rocks and cliffs backed off and allowed us more breathing room and most importantly, reaction time.

Cortez and the Ridgebacks were still marking ground at a good pace, and we and the mounts were doing our best to keep within hearing distance.

There was a noticeable wind that was becoming stronger out of the north and that could signal the coming of colder weather. Cold weather could come quickly at the elevation that we were positioned now.

In another hour, heavy clouds moved in on us and darkness began casting its veil for the night; it was time to make camp and arrange for the night.

We found a spot with plenty of dead larger brush that we could use to build a campfire with and settled in. It was no time until the pack animals were unloaded, and supper was in the skillets. We were on steaks cut from the second round of the big antelope by now and seared in the hot skillet, they were delicious; the skillet\-fried Irish potatoes sure complemented the meal.

The hard wind laid down leaving only a slight breeze just before it got time to turn in. Plenty of wood on the fire felt good as we blanketed up against the inner linings of our saddles and prepared for the cold night in the hills.

The camp was positioned so the rise of secondary boulders shielded us from a cutting north breeze, but during the night when I got up to relieve myself, I peeped from behind them and the north breeze almost took my breath away. I thought how cold it would be if the wind was really howling.

Morning found us drinking coffee and waiting on a hot breakfast before resuming the trail. The coffee that trip was as good as I have ever tasted; maybe it was the clear mountain stream water that caused it to taste so good.

The dogs feasted on antelope carcass trimmings as we grained the stock for the day's venture.

Everyone watered at the clear mountain stream before pulling out. With canteens filled, we positioned them on our mounts and pulled out.

Cortez and the Ridgebacks resumed the cat trail without asking them, as the rest of us tagged along behind; I had a pretty fair feeling that we would see action today.

About an hour on the trail, we found the body of a Stone Sheep that had been killed and covered with brush behind boulders overlooking the trail. we had made contact with our enemy.

It is common for the mountain lion to kill its prey and then hide it out, covered with brush, grass or limbs, to hide it until the cat returns to take it to the den. Some think that this amount of time allowed has a tenderizing effect on the carcass. I do not agree with that theory. If you have seen the mouth and especially the teeth of a mountain lion, you would readily agree that nothing needs to be tenderized for them to consume it.

A hidden carcass can be a varying distance from the den. I have observed such distances as far as almost a mile. In mountainous country, the distance is usually much shorter. In this case, we had to be near to our quarry.

We called the dogs off the carcass of the Stone Sheep, and they resumed the trail, moving higher as they continued on.

Elevation was becoming a deterrent for us now. We were moving slower, and it was increasingly getting harder to breathe.

About an hour before dark, we spotted a single large cat watching us from a ridge about 300 yards away. He was big and bold and was standing tall on higher ground; he was not afraid of anything.

I thought to myself that this cat must be enormous because even at this distance, without glass, it appeared huge. When the spotting scope was placed on him, it only reaffirmed what we already knew.

Those Kiamichi Mountain cats are hard to depict with the naked eye at 300 yards.

Harold wanted to take a shot, but I discouraged him because of the time involved of finding him after dark and it would be dark by the time we crawled to him.

"Harold, if he shows himself in the morning, you take the shot and we will have plenty of time to retrieve the body. I do not like to think of hunting for a possibly wounded cat after it gets dark, especially one that is this big," was my reply to him.

Harold placed his rifle back in its holster, and we started preparing to make camp. He kept looking at the big cat, and yes, he was still there; he had not moved.

I heard Harold, say in a low voice, "Stay right there Mr. Lion, and when daylight comes I will put a slug through you."

Harold watched him until he could see him no more. Darkness fell around us, and for the first night since we had been on the hunt, there was a sense of alarm in the air; we had lions close.

How close? We really did not know.

After another antelope steak and potato dinner, we turned in, but not until we built the fire up and secured plenty of debris to keep it going through the night. It was going to be another cold one; the moon had come out bright and hung over the eastern horizon.

An accomplished artist could not have done the scene justice. If it had not been for spotting the big cat before we pitched camp, we could have really enjoyed the setting. Now, there was too much apprehension amongst us as we turned in. We drew lots for guard duty with each hunter being assigned a 90-minute watch during the night. That offered some assurance that we could remain safe while affording us to rest a bit.

Regardless, my Smith and Wesson 44 Magnum, $8^3/_8$" barrel, laid in my hand against my chest as I dozed off. The last thought I had that night was of Cleve Welling and his Indian friend, Chelo, and the enormous cat that they had killed, many years ago, in the Gila Mountains.

His Indian friend, Chelo, was an Apache warrior and blood brother to Cleve Welling. He was also Geronimo's half-brother.

The story told of Chelo and Cleve dated back to a time when they were just young boys, growing up in the foothills of the mountains and doing what young boys did in preparation of becoming a man.

Chelo had been badly wounded when attacked by a mountain lion, and Cleve happened along at the right time and saved his life. It was such an adventurous story, and their friendship continued to grow.

That was another day and another story and besides, I was almost to the point of not remembering anything; sleep had come to me.

The next morning, as we were moving around the campground and preparing for the day, Harold handed me a cup of coffee and said, "The big cat is not on the ridge this morning. I was waiting for it to get light enough to see him, but when daylight came, he was not there."

"Harold, we need to divide our group of six into twosomes and position ourselves at a vantage point on the ridge that the big cat was on last night," I said. "By doing this, and remaining hidden, there is a great possibility that we could get a shot at a cat or two during the day.:

"We can stake the dogs in the shade from the nearby boulders and make our way to our positions before it gets too late in the day," I continued.

Harold liked the idea and took it from there by assigning the twosomes and sending the other two groups on their way. He elected to join me in the day's hunt.

Everyone took their gear, their guns, a sack of jerky and a canteen of cool water; it might be a long day on the boulders.

By mid-morning, everyone was in position to see most of the side of the mountain where he had spotted the big cat on the ridge the night before.

It was a clear day after the morning mountain haze finally burned off. The sun came out and everything started heating up, including the boulders we were sitting on.

It was a couple of hours into the afternoon when one group of hunters spotted a large cat on a boulder about 200 yards from them. As they watched the cat, another appeared with him. They had their spotting scopes on two different individuals and were watching them closely.

After several minutes, they determined that the cats did not see them but were watching another group of hunters.

Harold and I were too far removed down the western slope to observe the cats. We just sat and watched the part of the mountain that we could see.

Shots rang out, two to be exact. We knew that one of the groups had made contact with a mountain lion and had possibly scored a kill.

After several minutes of climbing, we were in a position to observe the other two groups of our friends. One group of hunters was moving toward an outer ridge and the other group was headed their way.

Harold and I followed suit until we found ourselves within speaking distance and learned that two big cats had been knocked down by the first group and they were on their way to claim their targets.

Upon arrival to the ridge that the cats were on when they were spotted and shot, we found our other two groups of hunters. Everyone was standing around two extremely large cats and were wowed by their size.

They were both male and each exceeded 200 pounds in weight.

After careful examination, I remarked to the group, "Friends, my hunt is over. I will not turn my dogs out on cats of this size and expect them to come back alive. When we get to camp, I will be ready to move back down the mountain with my dogs. If we are to continue hunting cats of this size, I recommend that we go to the steel traps."

The rest of the group agreed with me, and it was decided that we would retreat back to the base camp and decide on our method of trapping from there.

We moved back down the mountain range, with Harold and his younger brother falling behind to bring the largest of the dead cats with them. I knew they would have to have a picture of the unusual kill.

Could these cats be comparable to the big mountain lion that Cleve and Chelo killed many moons ago in the Gila Mountains?

After arrival at the base camp, we began getting our gear together. There was no more need for the dogs since I had seen the size of our prey.

I slowly began loading the dually for the long trip home. The animals sensed us preparing to return to the house, and I think they were happy that this hunt was nearing an end. Whether they knew it or not, they wanted no part of the Gila Mountain cats. It was my job to keep them separated. These size cats would have been hard to do anything with without getting my dogs seriously injured or killed. Shooting them, as we did, was the only way to eliminate them.

I look back today and ponder if I would have been involved with killing the huge mountain lions if I had felt the way about them that I feel now. My answer would probably be "no," I would not do it again. We didn't understand then that we were responsible for breaking an ecological chain, a chain that had been in place for thousands of years.

I told my amigos goodbye and that I would like to return to those mountains another trip with them and spend more time by the river. They agreed that would be nice and promised that we would plan it in the future.

They all waved as I pulled out, headed for the main road that would eventually deliver us to the interstate. Once there, we could settle in for the many miles that laid ahead of us.

Maybe, without any unforeseen problems, we would be home in a couple of days.

MARJORIE'S SHOW CALVES

I had been home for several months when Marjorie Bowles called and asked me if I would return to her ranch in The Texas Hill Country and help her and Walter select individual cows to artificial inseminate to raise next year's show calves that she would have for selection and sale.

Ever since she completely revamped her breeding program several years ago, her show calves had gotten better. Last season, her calves won three of the major shows across the southwest and placed second in that many more. Marjorie was establishing her name in the show calf business.

I told her that I would make a swing down that way in the next couple of weeks.

After I committed, she went on to say the pump at the windmill in the catch lot needed rebuilding while I was there. I smiled to myself and told her to have Walter order all the parts, and I would do it for her upon my return to her ranch.

When Marjorie asked, Marjorie received. That was the way it had always been with her. She had been way too nice to me down through the years, and I would remain indebted to her forever. After she was gone, I still owed her; that is just the way that she would have wanted to leave it.

She went on to tell me that some of the local cowboys were tie-down roping at her place two nights a week, on Tuesday and Thursday, and if I wanted to join in, I needed to bring Buck with me.

I told her I would. Deep down, I felt that she told me this to get me down there sooner. She did love when I returned to visit with them all; it was always a party when we got together.

One week from that day, I loaded the trailer early one morning. As I opened the rear gate, Buck stepped in as if he knew where we were going.

"All the way to the front Big Boy. We are going to Marjorie's for some roping," I said to him as he loaded.

After all my gear was loaded and I told Anita and the kids "goodbye," Buck and I hit the road south. We would pick up Highway 31 in Tyler and head to Waco. At Waco, we would hit Interstate 35 S toward Austin. From there I would exit toward Killeen and find my way to 281 S. That would take me to my turnoff in Blanco. I knew the way as well as I knew the back of my hand, and if the traffic was not too bad, I would be sitting in Marjorie's front yard in less than six hours.

When I got to her place, I drove over the cattle guard, and as I entered the yard, I pulled to the right and parked next to the Hill Country picket cedar post fence that she called her goat pen.

They met me as I got out, and my first words to them was, "When are we going to cook some cabrito?"

Walter hugged me and said, "We really have some fat wethers that would make some fine barbecue, my friend. We will have to ask Marjorie."

Marjorie grabbed me second and replied, "Get the pit hot. You do not have to ask me a thing about cooking goats. We will have a party if y'all want to."

After a long hug, she finally turned me loose and said, "Let's get you unloaded. Put your gear in the guest room and put Buck in the barn. The boys will grain him for you after they water him.

"Juanita has some sandwiches made and we were waiting for you to arrive before we ate," she said as we all walked toward the ranch house.

The hugging ritual was extended when Juanita laid eyes on me, and it seemed as if she had missed me as much as any of them. It was great to be back with my friends.

Juanita had the table spread with ham and pimento cheese sandwiches, an assortment of cheeses and pickles, with a glass of cold Hill Country sweet tea. It sure hit the spot after the long morning on the highway.

Along before dark, a heavy cloud formed back in the southwest, and it brought promise of a much-needed rain. It was not long until the thunder and lightning turned loose, and we all knew what was coming.

Walter and I pulled a yellow slicker on, from where they hung on the back porch, and made our way to the barn. I wanted to check on Buck and let him know that I was near while this storm blew through.

Walter and I sat on a couple of cane bottom chairs in the barn and listened while the disturbance howled on the outside. It was a nice warm place to stay out of the weather.

We chewed plug tobacco and talked about the ranch and the all the new stock brought on by the cross-breeding program that Marjorie had put in place several years before.

He knew how instrumental I had been in convincing Marjorie of making the genetic changes to improve the quality of livestock on her ranch.

After discussing many subjects, we finally got around to selecting the cross breeds that she was going to artificial inseminate to get the best individuals that were available to her.

Gelbvieh, Simmental and Chianina were the most popular breeds of the day, and they all were European Exotics.

It had been a customary practice for Marjorie to order 30 straws of frozen semen each year from prize bulls representing those breeds.

After the first two years, Marjorie was so pleased with the calves from the crosses, she began doubling up and breeding 60 females of her excellent F1 herds.

These were the F1 females that were a result of crossing her prized Herefords with McKellar's Zebu Brahman, a program that had really been successful.

It was mine and Walter's job to select the F1 female recipients for the coming year and to also, with Marjorie's assistance, select the individual sires we wanted to use on them.

Sixty straws of semen were expensive, and costs could run as high as $6,500.

It took us three days in the working pens, but we finally finished our selections and placed the donor tags in each individual ear, so we knew where each straw was going.

We were exactly 90 days from starting the year's artificial insemination breeding program. All the straws would be ordered and would be in place and kept in the liquid nitrogen tanks in the store room at the ranch.

In 45 days, the spotter bulls would be placed with the selected females. That would determine when it would be time to breed them. This was a busy time and Walter, along with three of his best ranch hands would almost be confined to the herd for the next several weeks, or until the last female had been bred.

Carnation had sent a technician to the ranch a couple of years ago that trained three of the ranch hands in palpation and insemination techniques. The cowboys had become very proficient in their work.

After my expertise, along with Walter's and Marjorie's, had been used for the selections, my work was done except for repairing the pump on the windmill in the catch lot.

Walter got all the parts for the rebuild out and helped me get the pump down to work on it early the next morning. After about three hours, the rebuild was complete and the pump was placed back in position to operate.

With one long smooth spin, she took off, pumping water as if she had never stopped. It was a time for rejoicing; water is crucial to raising livestock.

The last day I spent with them at the ranch was a really memorable occasion. Two of the ranch hands had cleaned six of the fat wethers, and I had spent the afternoon at the pit in the back yard preparing the meat.

Like always, Marjorie had another opportunity to entertain, and she and Juanita were not about let that go to waste.

There were about 60 guests present when they all arrived. It did not take Marjorie long to get a group together; sometimes I thought she kept them on standby.

The neighboring lady rancher that was the violin player in San Antonio was there. Her music was always so entertaining, played under the sprawling live oaks, on a late afternoon, in the Texas Hill Country; there was not a better place on earth to be.

The wethers turned out as delicious as anyone could have asked for. When young goats are processed, it is of the utmost importance to skin them and keep the hair off of the edible meat. Unusual tastes come from the hair being allowed to touch the meat.

The Hispanic guys who processed the wethers did an outstanding job in keeping the meat uncontaminated. When they finished, I had them chunk up the carcasses and place them into wash pots for boiling. The chunks of young goat were slowly cooked until the meat became tender and started pulling away from the bone.

The long pit was fired, and the chunks of meat were placed on it for the final cooking. After a couple of hours at 325 degrees, a thin sauce was used to start, and it was brushed on about every 15 minutes until the cooking was done.

An hour later, all the bone was moved from the cabrito and only left the meat to continue receiving the brushes of sop.

Along with the chunks of cabrito, 25 chicken halves were placed over the coals to begin their cooking. Marjorie always liked to have at least two meat options when we were serving anything new or different.

Cabrito was neither new or different to people of that part of the world. It had been a cultural standby around most homesteads for centuries.

After about five hours and a bunch of sopping, the meat was ready to pull from the pit, rest it for a short time, and then slice it for the party.

The chicken halves had been placed on the pit at a time they might cook about three and a half hours before calling them done. The same barbecue sauce was used to sop them during the cooking process.

The following sauce is what I used for the cabrito and chicken. Over the years and all the cooking with it, I have found none any better.

BAR-BE-CUE SAUCE

1-quart vinegar
3 tablespoon black pepper
3 lemons (cross sectioned about $1/4$ inch)
1 small can paprika
2 large bottles catsup
1 bottle garlic salt
1 large Lea and Perrin Sauce (Worchestershire)
2 sticks Oleo
$1/2$ gallon water
2 large onions

1 cup sugar (brown sugar for a darker sauce)

This is a cooking sop. It makes 1$\frac{1}{2}$ gallons.

Mix all ingredients and let it cook slowly until lemons are tender. Salt to taste.

This recipe was passed on to Jim L. Richardson by an old black gentleman (Lovee Walker) in Camp County, Texas in 1964.

Barefoot, Mr. Walker would work around the hot pit all day in preparation for many a celebration in the area. He was the fire stoker and chief "sopper" for C.R. Guest, and his food was delicious.

Cecil Guest finally offered the recipe to me a short time before he passed away. I did not have the heart to tell him I had had it for years.

.   .   .

The next morning, bright and early, I left Marjorie's ranch and headed back home.

She had Walter and one of the cowboys load a 1,200-pound Simmental crossed steer on the trailer with Buck and told me to have him processed for my freezer. She thought that would be a surprise to me, but it was not uncommon for her to do something like that every time I visited the ranch.

I gave all of them a long hug goodbye before I crawled up into the dually and made my way to the main highway. In my rearview mirror, they were all there once again, waving goodbye.

With no trouble on the road, I would be back home in five to six hours. The road provided me with plenty of time to think, and that is mostly what I did as I pushed north.

The plate of oatmeal raisin cookies that Juanita had baked and placed in the front seat of the truck made the trip even better.

The 1,200-pound steer was dropped off at the meat processor, and I told him it might be a couple of weeks, but when I got back into town I would come out and get it.

To my surprise, when the steer was ready for pick-up, I had almost 750 pounds of top quality meat for the freezer.

We had some great steaks to take camping with us, a large brisket to smoke, not to mention the two large racks of ribs. It would be just right for the holidays.

LET'S GO CAMPING

When I arrived at home, Anita mentioned that she wanted to take the fifth wheel and kids and go to Arkansas camping for a few days. The following day, we lit out for the mountains and ended up just outside of Hot Springs at a quaint little mountain campground.

Lake Catherine, on the edge of Hot Springs is such a picturesque place to visit and spend some time there. Many things to do and many places to see are abundant in that locale.

We spent about three days there and then moved down to Daisy State Park at Narrows Dam. I have never been to any spot in Arkansas that was not beautiful. Narrows offers such a beautiful deep lake that is as scenic from the shore line as it is from the lake.

We had such a ball, camping and cooking out, that it was hard to return home after the ten days in the hills.

Our fifth wheel was a 40-footer, but it was before slides were placed in them. It was large and slept six people and was more than adequate for our family.

We pulled it with a '74 GMC ¾ ton that had an extra 50-gallon fuel tank in the bed of the truck. With all the tanks full, our range was somewhere between 1,100 and 1,200 miles, depending on the elevations we were traveling over.

We pulled it several times to Tennessee and Georgia along with other states in the southwest.

ANOTHER TRIP
DOWN TO MARJORIE'S RANCH

Monday morning found me at Marjorie's again. She had invited me and a friend down to visit with her for about a week and help work some of the crossbred cattle.

Later in the week, upon Juniper's Knoll, the two of us sat and discussed all that we had experienced together down through the years that I had been coming to her ranch. Many of the things we spoke of were the same subjects that seemed to come up every time we sat on the benches overlooking the river and talked.

Marjorie reminded me of the story of Tom that I had written and how the two of us had met at his family graveyard, many years ago down by the river.

That led into a long discussion of him and his family and his love for our country. We both agreed that his patriotism was second to no one.

Tom had a falling out with his grandfather one summer and had come over and asked Marjorie for a job. After about a month, Tom and his grandfather patched up their differences, but Tom was not allowed to quit the job that he had asked for.

Finally, when school started in the fall, he was allowed to move out of Marjorie's bunk house and move back home.

Marjorie said that the grandfather's persistency about the matter really surprised her. She had offered to release Tom from his obligation, but his grandfather would not allow him to quit.

Marjorie summed it all up for us when she said, "I did not understand grandfather's reasoning back then, but now, after the way Tom gave his life for his country and the commitment he had for everything that he loved, I better understand. He was a great young man, and it is no telling how far he would have gone in life."

Listening to her tell the story about Tom made me glad all over again that I had the privilege of calling him my friend.

Later that evening, in front of the fire, Marjorie asked me to read for her the story, My Friend Tom, one more time. I walked into my bedroom and retrieved it from the briefcase that contained all of my writings. I never went anywhere without them back in those days.

When I returned with the story, I sat down next to

her on the long couch, cleared my throat, and began to read it aloud.

I paused twice, with tears in my eyes, to also find Marjorie crying along with me. What a friend I did have in her.

Then, I was finished, and we sat and looked at each other for a while.

She was looking at me when she said, "Jim, that has to be my favorite story of all the ones you have written."

I shook my head in agreement with her and said, "Mine too, Marjorie. It does hit home for both of us, doesn't it?"

I had to include the original story:

MY FRIEND TOM

It was Wednesday before Spring Break '67, and I had not decided what to do during the week off. Some friends of mine had invited me to go snow skiing in Colorado. Another group was planning a bash on the beach at Galveston during the holidays.

I had not committed to either party, but I definitely

wanted to get out of Denton, Texas for a few days.

At last resort, I knew I could go home. I would enjoy seeing and visiting with my family, but I did not really want to go home because my father did not consider my time off, holidays, and he would find something for me to do on the farm. There was always equipment needing repair, fences to mend, or cattle to work.

My best friend, Tom, called just before dark and asked me if I had made any plans for the vacation from school. He told me to pack my gear, and we would spend a week in the Texas Hill Country, matching hunting prowess with the renowned Rio Grande turkey.

His grandfather owned a ranch on the Pedernales River and the hunting there was tremendous. Being familiar with that country, I knew what was in store for me and more than welcomed the invitation.

We had spent the previous Thanksgiving holidays with his grandparents and had hunted deer, turkey and quail on the ranch.

I knew the upcoming week was going to be much more than a hunting trip. The scenery on the ranch was so peaceful it would almost leave a newcomer, visiting there, in a trance.

After Tom's parents were killed in a car wreck in 1952, his grandparents raised him. Tom was a small boy of five when the tragedy struck. With the aid of family pictures, he could faintly remember the short period of time he had with his parents before their untimely death.

They too, along with the rest of his ancestors, were buried in the family plot, midst a live oak grove, down by the river.

Tom was sixth-generation and four of the previous generations were at rest in that cemetery, overlooking the river. He was an in-line descendant of pioneer stock which settled what is today known as the Texas Hill Country.

The same blood flowing in his veins had fought the Lipan Apaches and the Comanches. His great-great-grandfather had fought with General Sam Houston at San Jacinto and was present at the capture of General Antonio Lopez de Santa Anna.

The deep-rooted family pride ran rampant, and it was easily detected in the paraphernalia around the old ranch house.

Like always, his grandparents looked forward to seeing us, and the hospitality they extended to me was ever so gracious.

His grandmother was what every grandmother

should be. She was a splendid cook, and her black skillet biscuits, cactus preserves, and jalapeno jelly could not be touched by any gourmet chef in New York City.

Their spacious home once again welcomed me and absorbed me in its warmth and natural beauty. The old ranch house had been built in 1880 and was ten years old when Tom's grandfather was born.

The hunting trip was just as I expected it to be. We arrived at the ranch on Friday night and were in the field by five-thirty the next morning, concealed in a hastily made blind, awaiting the crafty turkeys to make their move from roost to feed.

Surrounded by prickly pear and covered with camouflage paint and clothing, we sat ever so quiet and waited for the first signs of breaking day.

These times, just before day, in the field and on lakes were some of the most pleasant moments Tom and I shared. The new day is always filled with hope and reassurance of good things to come; many times, they do come.

Like on most hunting and fishing trips, the time just before sun-up can be the most peaceful. Tom loved this time of the day as much as I did and often, back at school, we spoke of times such as these and how much we enjoyed sharing them together. The fellowship we had with each other during such times can never be replaced. They will live as a memory within me forever.

In a distance, we could see the sun as it began to cast rays of early morning light and bounce them off the Pedernales River. With each passing moment, the vast range began to show more of itself.

From a live oak grove to the south of us, we began to hear the turkeys as they left their roosts. From past experience, Tom knew the birds would leave their roost, fly down to the river for a drink and then they would meticulously begin gleaning the hillside below our blind.

This particular morning was no exception, and in less than an hour each of us bagged a nice gobbler.

We could have taken more, but neither of us ever measured our hunting and fishing success in numbers. Being there for a while just to enjoy all of it was ample reward for both of us.

Times as this cause me to contemplate about the poor souls who never take the time or have the opportunity to experience such an event.

Traveling back to the ranch house, we stopped by the family cemetery, overlooking the river. We visited the graves that contained my friend's rich heritage.

We have no way of knowing what the future holds and even if I had I would never have believed that in nineteen short months Tom would be lying there beneath the live oaks, overlooking the river.

Duty called him, just as it had called his ancestors. Unfortunately, unselfishly, Tom answered the summons and agreed to fight a war that was not his war. It was a war as foreign to him as the East Texas Piney Woods.

The Vietnam conflict was hot in 1966 and was getting even hotter. Watching the newscasts on television each night and seeing the body bags being unloaded at Love Field would cause my friend to often talk of being needed over there.

There were many other students our age with college deferments, but Tom never did feel comfortable with it. His ancestors had fought the Apaches, the Comanches, the Spaniards, the Mexicans, and were engaged in two World Wars. What was a little skirmish in Southeast Asia compared to all these?

Finally, in June 1968, Tom threw in and gave his part for what free men believe in. It was his way, and to understand his way you would had to have known my friend.

He was the type of person that developed "goose bumps" when the flag went by or when the national anthem was played or sung.

Like so many of his other attributes, the patriotism he displayed came natural and unrestrained.

November 12, 1968, while on patrol, Tom and several more in his unit were killed. Southeast Asia is a long way from the Texas Hill Country until something like this happens.

Men like my friend Tom are the ones who have helped make our nation great. I am forever grateful to have known him for even so short a time. I am thankful for his kind. God bless their souls. They are the true Patriots.

Without men like Tom, Old Glory would not fly today, free in the breeze and proud of all who have given the ultimate sacrifice to keep her that way.

Without such individuals, there would be no freedom of choice that so many of us take for granted.

Without Tom, sometimes I feel that part of myself has gone too. Without my friend, the Texas Hill Country will never quite be the same.

When I finished reading the story and the two of us regained our composure, we spoke once again of how fine a man Tom had become.

I spoke in terms of how much I loved and respected him for his patriotism and his love for our flag.

"All the time that I was around him, I never thought of him turning out to be a hero," Marjorie remarked.

My response was a simple, "I guess that is what made him such a hero; he was definitely our hero.

"Regardless, I wish the two of us could make that old Sonic drag down University Boulevard in Denton, Texas one more time," I added.

It was getting late in the evening and Juanita had stuck her head in the door and said that my room was ready for the night. I reminded Marjorie of how many times I had told Juanita not to worry with my bed, that I would take care of it. After all these years, she still does it.

Marjorie's response was, "Jim, she really likes you and if she did not, she would not care whether your bed was turned back or not. Juanita considers you as part of our family."

"A higher compliment, I could never be paid, and I am going to tell her about it," I answered.

"She would like that, my friend," Marjorie said, as she never looked up from what she was doing.

I smiled to myself and such a warm feeling broke over me; it is wonderful to be among friends.

The next morning at breakfast, I walked up to Juanita, gave her a huge hug and told her how much I appreciated everything that she did for me and the little extra things that she did to make me feel welcome when I visited the ranch.

She hugged me back and gave me a big kiss on the cheek.

Marjorie looked at us both, standing there in the kitchen hugging, and just gave us a long smile.

That look that she gave us still warms my heart to this day. Can a value be placed on the memories?

.　　　.　　　.

HUSH PUPPIES

This following hush puppy recipe is the one that I used whenever I prepared fried fish or mountain scallops. In all of my travels, I have found none better.

It is straight from the legendary catfish eating restaurant near Caddo Lake, Big Pines Lodge.

After trying them, I am sure that you will agree.

This is the only recipe that I ever used because of its consistency. The secret is using the cold buttermilk as cold as you can get it and having the grease just the right temperature. Too hot and they will overbrown on the outside and not be completely done on the inside. I always strived to maintain a temperature between 325-350 degrees.

Hot grease that will ignite a wooden kitchen match is usually just what you are looking for.

From the banks of Big Cypress Creek to the Ft. Worth Stockyards and the thousands of people that I have fed along the way, I share it with you.

Enjoy.

I have had observers, after drinking several beers,

stand and eat hush puppies dipped in my tartar sauce and get so full that they never consumed any of the main meal. Yes, they did swear by these hush puppies.

BIG PINES HUSH PUPPIES

$1/2$ cup corn meal
$1/2$ cup flour
$1/2$ teaspoon baking soda
$1/2$ teaspoon salt
$2/3$ cup buttermilk
1 egg
Chopped onions

Mix and spoon into hot deep fryer.

SULPHUR RIVER HUSH PUPPIES

Flour
Yellow cornmeal
White onion
Evaporated milk
Cooking oil
Baking powder
Salt
Eggs

Ice water
Mix 1 cup flour, 1 cup cornmeal, 2 teaspoons baking powder, ½ teaspoon salt, 1 cup white onion chopped fine, ¼ cup sugar.

Mix ingredients well.

Add ¼ cup cooking oil and two eggs.

Add ½ evaporated milk and ½ ice water until mixture becomes a thick paste.

Roll puppies out in hand or drop from spoon into hot grease.

Cook until golden brown and floating.

Hint: If puppy is too large it will not cook all the way through.

Remove and drain on paper towel.

A PUPPY RECIPE WITH CORN

Another "corn puppy" recipe:

1 cup Pioneer biscuit mix
1 can cream style corn

Add, according to personal preference the

following: green onions, onion, and/or jalapenos.

Mix thoroughly and drop by spoon into hot grease.

You may want to try these. They will not disappoint you at all.

1½ cup plain cornmeal
½ cup self-rising flour
1½ teaspoon baking powder
½ teaspoon salt

Boil water.

Add water and stir until the meal is completely wet – not runny, but consistently moistened (this cooks the cornmeal); it will be like playdough.

When it cools enough, start rolling into shapes.

Quick freeze on a cookie sheet.

Bring cooking oil to 325-350 degrees and drop in frozen hush puppies.

Options: chopped onion and jalapenos can be added just before boiling water.

Make and freeze in advance – they will keep.

MRS. ADA'S CHRISTMAS DIVINITY

Mrs. Ada, in the Oklahoma Panhandle, was not one to make use of the kitchen very often. She had her coffee there every morning about 4:30 or 5:00.

She could be found at the kitchen table if she was trying to repair something that took skill and patience. She would dig out her small set of screwdrivers and other tools, turn on a bright lamp and work diligently until her task was complete.

It was four days before Christmas one year, and she had ordered a new Redfield scope for her 270 Winchester. She was busy at the kitchen table trying to get the base plate mounted.

She looked at me and commented that she had shot through Redfield scopes for many years and really liked them. She said that once the scope was mounted and sighted in, it would hold its settings. Later that morning after sunrise, we went out and sighted it in.

She shot it three times and had it on the money. That was my friend...as tough as the Panhandle wind.

These were the only times you could find her in the kitchen except when she moved Juanita aside to make her Christmas Divinity. She loved her divinity and gave much of it away during Christmas. She was proud when I asked her for the recipe.

$2^2/_3$ cups sugar
$^1/_2$ cup water
1 teaspoon vanilla
$^1/_2$ teaspoon salt
$^1/_2$ cup white Karo
2 egg whites
$^1/_2$ cup black walnuts

Mrs. Ada used black walnuts from large walnut trees in the back yard. She said that any nuts would do and occasionally used chopped pecans.

Boil sugar, water, syrup and salt in a saucepan until a drop in cold water forms a hard ball.

Pour over stiffly beaten egg whites in a thin stream. Add vanilla and continue to beat until stiff. Fold in nuts. Pour in pan lined with wax paper. When set, cut in squares.

COUNTRY SWEET POTATO PIE

Large sweet potatoes
Nutmeg
Cinnamon
Brown sugar
Ginger
Vanilla
Softened stick butter
Evaporated milk
Eggs
Salt
Pastry shells
White sugar

In a covered Dutch oven, bake two large sweet potatoes until they are soft, with the syrup running out of the ends.

Place peeled, cooled-down sweet potatoes in a large mixing bowl. Should be at least 4 cups worth.

Add 2 sticks softened butter, 2 cups brown sugar, $1/2$ teaspoon salt, 1 teaspoon ginger, 1 teaspoon nutmeg (or allspice), 2 teaspoons cinnamon, 4 eggs, 1 cup evaporated milk, and $1/2$ cup white sugar.

Blend thoroughly with 1 teaspoon vanilla.

Fill pre-baked pie shells and bake at 350 degrees

until pie is solid. Makes two pies.

Set on a flaky crust. There is none better to a connoisseur of the East Texas sweet potato.

During my years as a hunter, I was always notorious for finding the best sloughs and erecting the best blinds for concealment from the migratory game birds.

Being referred to as a "slough hunter" fit me to a tee.

OXBOW SLOUGHS

With it being cold and wintry last night, it called for a roaring fire in the big room. As I sat in my recliner and read Nash Buckingham, my attention was drawn to the reflecting heat from the stove.

The coals were red hot, just as they had been around many a campfire during my lifetime. I sat there in all that comfort, and the rusty reels in my mind began to run. They ran back in time to places and friends that shared company with me. I closed my eyes and once again heard the laughter of the groups.

On that particular evening I was magically drawn back to an oxbow slough along the Sulphur River where we set trotlines for the famous Sulphur River channel cats and at times, caught the white perch. Bountiful stringers were harvested down through the years, and many families were fed from the slough's offerings.

I cannot even start to count the boatloads of fish and game that were removed from those bottoms.

There was a group of us that enjoyed the campfires and hunted and fished together there for many seasons. We would make a camp on the bank and spend two to three days at a time in that locale. The fishing and fellowship were wonderful.

My mind wandered back to an extremely cold Christmas Eve morning and a duck hunt on the slough. It was snowing, and there was ice everywhere. We had the blocks set, and they were working in the wind.

Our group of hunters was concealed in a heavily-caned blind overlooking the decoys. First flight appeared just after daylight and legal shooting time. The hunt was on, and it remained so for several hours. Flights of northern mallards and pintails just kept coming.

We all bagged our limits and that was back when limits were much larger than they are today.

We were cold and tired, and the dogs were worn out. We waded back to the bank and built a fire from some covered wood that we were saving for that purpose. As we sat around the fire and warmed ourselves, a large bottle of blueberry brandy was passed around.

The stories ran freely, and with each passing of the jug, they got louder. As the dogs rested in their boxes on soft hay, we continued reminiscing about the hunt and previous hunts.

The temperature was falling by afternoon and the snow thickened. After a while we all loaded up our gear and headed the trucks out of the bottom.

I want to return to that oxbow slough off the Sulphur River. Most of the time it holds a flight of Christmas ducks. It has been many years since I have been there and hunted it.

I think I will leave out early Christmas morning, before the grandkids get up and open their presents, and sit quietly while watching for that first flight.

I know they will come.

CREEK BANKS AND COOKING SOCIALS

I cannot bypass this opportunity of telling about all the stews, chili cooking, barbecues and other meals that were enjoyed along the banks of the creeks in Northeast Texas as I was growing up and living life to the fullest, with my dear friends.

This following recipe comes to my mind when I mentally return to those days.

A slight chill on the air with leaves beginning to fall was only added enticement for each of us. We referred to it as "jacket weather."

I guess an overall favorite recipe was a wash pot full of the following stew.

PINEY WOODS CHICKEN STEW

Whole chickens
White potatoes (firm)
White onions
Salt
Garlic powder
Carrots
Greek salad peppers
Cajun seasoning
Red pepper
Tomatoes
Pepper

Paprika
Whole kernel corn
Tomato sauce
Oregano

Boil chickens until meat will peel easily from the bone. Debone and place meat in a wash pot. Cover with broth. Sprinkle with oregano.

Add onions and cook until they become transparent. Add cut up tomatoes and tomato sauce. Stir in some salt, pepper, paprika and garlic powder. Set aside to simmer.

Cut up potatoes and boil them until they start to soften (do not overcook). Drain off liquid until it barely covers potatoes. Add canned carrots.

Add Greek salad peppers and whole kernel corn. Peppers should float on top, and corn should be added just before the final simmer starts. I always just loved to pour the peppers right out of the bottle across the top of the stew; we all knew then that we were almost finished.

Simmer with a tablespoon of red pepper and ½ cup of Tony Chachere's Cajun Seasoning.
Hint: Corn will go to the bottom and burn if heat is too high. That is why it is added at the start of the final simmer.

This stew recipe was prepared in an old wash pot,

stirred with a boat paddle, served and enjoyed numerous times with a multitude of close friends at a primitive camp site on a Caddo Indian mound, overlooking Big Cypress Creek Bottom in Camp County, Texas.

Fond memories of those friends and socials still linger.

CHANGES

Now as I have grown older, and most of the triviality of my childhood dreams have long been forgotten, there are times when I wish it were possible for me to return and relive some of those younger days.

Every now and then, and recently more often, my mind wanders back to such times, when things were different. Times when we all had more time for each other and everyone was not as hurried, headed nowhere.

Those were days long ago, when we took the time to help a friend or neighbor in need. It was a time when we would visit with our fellow man and sit on the front porch, and we would not hesitate until all differences were talked out. Lawyers starved to death back in those days.

Those were times we thought, at the time, would never change and would remain that way forever. That was before we became aware that life itself is such a fleeting moment. That was the time when we thought Mom and Dad would live forever and would always be there for us.

Occasionally, in nostalgic dreams, I return to those wonderful, carefree days and revisit the people and places that I hold so dear in my memories.

These dreams come more often now and are consistently drawn to the simple things of those times long past. Time has a way of changing everything, and some of the things I once thought important have taken on different perspectives.

As a youngster growing up, I could not wait to get away from home and my hometown. I had big schemes and dreams to fulfill and endless roads to travel and the highest mountains with distant peaks to climb.

"The grass is always greener on the other side of the fence" certainly applied to me at this stage of my life. As age brought on maturity, I abandoned most of my childish whims.

I climbed tall mountains and visited many new places and made a multitude of friends in between. But somehow, in all my travels and adventures, I yearned for the place that I fought so desperately to leave. Home is a place filled with people you love and really care about because you know deep down how much they care about you.

I am convinced now, being in my autumn years and with much greater skills of contemplation, that we, as individuals, change and these changes are as dramatic as the effect of time.

BAYOU DUMPLINGS

Chicken
Milk
Buttermilk
Chicken bouillon granules
Garlic Salt
Paprika
Baking powder
Corn starch
Onion flakes
Corn
English peas
Flour
Poultry seasoning, ground red pepper, black pepper (coarse), parsley flakes, onions or shallots, crushed red pepper, Louisiana Hot Sauce

Prepare dumplings first. Combine 2 cups flour, $2^1/_2$ teaspoons baking powder, 1 cup buttermilk (well shaken), salt, pepper, $^1/_2$ teaspoon ground red pepper, and add 1 teaspoon of paprika. Mix well and thicken or thin with either flour or buttermilk. Pour out on floured surface, flour top and roll out to a desired (I prefer $^1/_4$" to $^3/_8$") thickness. Cut into $1^1/_2$" squares.

In a large covered pan, cover chicken (fat hen recommended) with water (at least 6 cups). Cook until meat falls off the bone. Cool, remove skin, debone, cut up or tear apart, and submerge back into the liquid the chicken was cooked in.

Add I cup of chopped onion (I prefer shallots), I teaspoon poultry seasoning, 1 tablespoon onion flakes, 3 teaspoons chicken bouillon granules, $1\frac{1}{2}$ teaspoon Louisiana Hot Sauce, $\frac{1}{2}$ teaspoon crushed red pepper, $\frac{1}{2}$ teaspoon ground red pepper, 1 teaspoon garlic salt, and bring to a rolling boil (stirring occasionally) for 5 minutes.

Combine 2 cups milk, 2 tablespoons corn starch, and 1 cup flour. Place in a jar with lid and shake until mixture is smooth. Add mixture to rolling boil, stirring constantly until mixture begins to thicken.

Cut heat to a simmer.

Drop cut dumplings into mixture, gently turn them in, shake parsley and paprika generously over the top and simmer with the lid on for approximately 15 minutes. Add peas and corn last. Corn will stick to the bottom and scorch if added too early.

Momma Debut, God bless her soul, is famous for many things and this dish is one of them. It is still popular all over her parish.

When her son, Joe, and I would return from the

swamps after a good hunt or successful fishing trip, it was always such a welcomed sight to see Momma, waiting for us at the back door, with Bayou Dumplings on the table. Frequently we chased those dumplings with her renowned buttermilk pie.

I named her recipe Bayou Dumplings instead of chicken dumplings because of the spiced-up taste and the fact that Momma would sometimes use a soft-shell turtle, a cut up "gator" chop, or a guinea, as a substitute for a fat hen.

This recipe has a mild heat to it, and it can be altered as you desire. It will become a favorite in most groups.

A WILD GAME MEAT MARINADE

Vegetable oil
Thyme
Garlic
A-1 Steak Sauce
Salt
Pepper (coarse ground)
Paprika
Worchestershire Sauce
Heinz Steak Sauce

In a container, mix 15 ounces vegetable oil, 3 ounces Worchestershire Sauce, 3 ounces. Heinz Steak Sauce, 3 ounces A-1 Steak Sauce, 2 bunches of fresh chopped thyme, 16 minced garlic cloves, 4 teaspoons black pepper and 1 tablespoon salt.

Pour over meat and refrigerate until ready to cook.

Works great on all meat. Especially good on elk, deer, wild boar and bear.

Hint: Cold salt water purges all dressed game. Process the meat and let it sit in cold salt water for a few hours.

High Eagle, a Mescalero Apache of New Mexico, shared this with me on a bear hunt in 1974. The mescal "squeezings" were our libations, and we smoked the peace pipe. I was much younger then and not nearly as wise.

FOR THE LOVE OF BARBECUE

I had a dear friend in South Dallas who had been raised in my small hometown before he broke out and sought his worldly claim under the bright lights of the city.

He had a barbecue joint down on Illinois Avenue, and during the summer I would haul him load after load of big Carolina Cross watermelons to sell at his place. They would average about 60-75 pounds each

I arrived mid-morning, and a large bob-tail truck trailer of the melons would last about one afternoon on his parking lot.

Not only watermelons, he also had me bring as many of the famous Pittsburg Hot Links that I could get the hot link cookers to have ready when I left town headed to Illinois Avenue. My excursions to his place of business involved five or six trips a week when the market was hot.

In return, I ate some of the best original Black Man Barbecue in the world and drank some of the coldest beer I ever swallowed.

I never went hungry around him, and the sauce

was so good that I could stand around the pit while he cooked and eat nothing but "sop sandwiches."

He called his barbecue sauce "Come Back".

COME BACK BARBECUE SAUCE

$1/2$ gallon water (approximately)
3 white onions (large)
6-10 chopped green onions or shallots
2 cups brown sugar darkened in a skillet
2 cups of concentrated lemon juice
$1/2$ quart vinegar
$3/4$ cup salt
2 cups of raw honey
3 cans of premium beer
4 tablespoons black pepper
1 tablespoon ground red pepper
I small bottle garlic salt
2 tablespoons chili powder
3 large bottles of Worchestershire Sauce
8 lemons (cross sectioned about $1/4$ inch)
1 large can paprika
10 large cans tomato sauce

Thoroughly mix all ingredients and let cook slow until lemons are tender. Add or delete ingredients according to individual taste.

Sauce can be thinned by adding $1/2$ vinegar and $1/2$ water.

A thinner sauce is recommended when using as a sop.

This was served on many occasions to a multitude of friends and acquaintances throughout our "neck of the woods."

This recipe was borrowed from a friend in South Dallas. He says, "Try me one time and I got you."

I truly loved this man and readily admit that after World War II, when he settled in Dallas and had the guts and integrity to leave our small town in order to better himself, that his life has been one of the biggest success stories that I have ever witnessed.

No college for my friend; he was too busy trying to make a living when he returned home from the war. His life was honed by hard knocks as he strived every day to pull himself up and raise his family. In my eyes, he was a total success.

Who knows? My next book may be centered around him and his colorful life.

This recipe is on the shelves under a different name. He is gone now, but the sauce has been marketed for years and has been very successful.

Not too long ago, I had reason to be back down in South Dallas and was not too far from Illinois Avenue. Yes, I did take the time to drive by the location where my friend served his famous barbecue for many years.

The extra time that I took to go by his place amply rewarded me. He was on my mind for the next several days; those thoughts prompted me adding him to this book.

SUNSET MAGIC

By choice, like so many times before, I chose to fish on past the witching hour. The witching hour is known to all outdoorsmen as that magical lapse of time between sunset and total darkness.

To the avid duck hunter, it is the period after legal shooting time when all the surroundings get quiet again and the hunter looks up from gathering his decoys to find the sky full of ducks, when only moments before there was not one in sight.

The witching hour is the time of day when strange things can happen, and most of the time they do. It is during this time when the wise moss-back buck finally shows himself. There is barely enough light through the scope to make him out, and the antlers on his head can be as large as any imagination.

During the witching hour, the bucket mouth bass comes from the deep to explode on the same top water plug that was ignored all afternoon.

Yes indeed, such times only happen during the witching hour. These moments are golden, and they are covered with twinkle dust as they fall through the hourglass with much more expediency than we would like for them to.
These are the times I cherish and would like to hold onto forever, knowing all along that it is impossible to do so. Deeply etched in my mind are

the countless hours I have spent on a lake or in the field through the sunset of another day.

This time of the day can be the equalizer for the sportsman who has spent a hard day hunting or fishing. Alone on a lake during such times holds ample rewards for me. It is sometimes during this time when I feel cold chills run up my spine, and I can almost hear voices of individuals who have gone this way before me. Past experiences during such times have made me feel closer to primitive man.

My thoughts wandered to times past as I tried to imagine what early man thought when he witnessed such a closure at the end of day. Perhaps his thoughts were similar to mine as he beheld the glorious creation of our God. Perhaps he felt as I felt and wondered if man before him had the same feelings.

Could it have been feelings such as these that inspired the markings that are preserved on the walls of his cave?

On this particular evening, I witnessed one of the most beautiful sunsets ever placed on the trestle board of life. I felt as if God's artistry that evening was for me alone. I could not keep from thinking how anyone could behold such magnificence and still make atheistic professions.

Nature has such a way of inspiring me. It sets my mind in motion and often creates feelings that are difficult to explain. The splendor of a sunset is a reminder to be thankful to God for letting me spend another day in His world.

It was completely dark by the time I put the fishing equipment in the rod box. After securing other items and fastening my life vest, I cranked the big Evinrude and slowly began exiting the cove.

A late flight of wood ducks whistled over my head as they made their way to a flooded roost.

Along the water's edge, a great horned owl glided above the reed tops, in search of an evening meal.

From a shoreline, in shallow water, a blue heron scolded me as if to remind me I had spent too much time where I was not wanted.

High over my head, a triple "vee" of nomadic geese continued their pilgrimage to the bountiful rice fields along the coast.

By now I reached the big water and with a flick of my finger, the running lights came on. As the bass boat planed out and the powerful engine hummed behind me, I began to sing to myself.

"Oh, Lord my God, when I in awesome wonder,

consider all the world Thy hands have made. I see the stars, I hear the rolling thunder, Thy power throughout the universe displayed. Then sings my soul . . . "

IT IS WILDFLOWER TIME AGAIN
IN THE TEXAS HILL COUNTRY

I woke up this morning with Marjorie Bowles on my mind. It has been thirty-seven years since I sat with her, on Juniper's Knoll, overlooking the Pedernales River, watched her wildflowers in bloom, scattered forever across the landscape, and just visited with my friend.

I purposely laid in bed a while this morning and yearned for the pleasant dreamed visit with Marjorie to last just a little bit longer before I fully awoke.

After I finally got up, turned on the laptop and drank my coffee, Marjorie kept whispering to me to go ahead; "Go ahead Jim, and write that story about our wildflowers…you know how much we loved them."

Many a year ago, before I ever visited her beautiful ranch back in the '80s, she had Walter, one of her ranch hands, build a Bois d'arc planked bench for her to sit there on the knoll and pass her time, sometime in deep contemplation and other times just enjoying her beautiful wildflowers.

The bench was placed near three small live oak trees, and it was about a two-hundred-yard stroll from Marjorie's front porch to the top of the knoll where the bench rested beneath the trees.

My trips to her ranch varied, but I was usually there with her during the fall of the year and especially the spring turkey season just as the Texas Bluebonnets and Indian Paintbrushes were really showing off their magnificence.

After my first visit in 1980 and the way I carried on about her bench and the beautiful hillside and wildflowers scattered over it, Marjorie had Walter build another bench, just for me. She must have been excited because she even called me that very night and told me what she had done.

After that, I never returned to her ranch that we did not take the time and walk up on top of the knoll and sit on the benches; especially during spring turkey season.

Later, she broadcast some Crimson Clover seed along the river and around the outskirts of the wildflowers, and when it bloomed, the blossoms were blood red and set everything off.

As we walked along up the hill, Marjorie would carry a gallon galvanized foot tub about half full of milo and would scatter it for the wild turkey. The trek was a ritual with her and usually she did it twice a day; first, early in the morning and second, during the waning part of the day.

Sometimes, as she walked along scattering the grain, she could stop and look back and see the turkeys following along at a distance, eating the milo.

"Jim, they have tamed to the point of not even knowing that I am watching them," she remarked as we paused and watched.

As the years rolled by and we became closely acquainted, her little spot up on Juniper's Knoll became an area that I held dear in my heart. I can close my eyes this morning and still see it in all its splendor.

I can breathe deeply and smell all the wonderful fragrances of the flowers; their memory is still there, and it is still as strong as the day I first smelled them. They are a constant reminder that it is the small things in life that sometimes offer us the largest treasures.

I can close my eyes and once again and hear the buzzing of the Hill Country honey bees as they collect nectar from the wild flowers, the clover and the honey locust blossoms.

The grandeur of it all came so natural to me as I would sit, listening to Marjorie tell about the ranch she was raised on and how much her ancestors had loved it.

With time, they all passed on; Marjorie stayed. In time, Marjorie's parents, who spent their lifetime ranching there, passed on; Marjorie stayed.

Now, it was all Marjorie's alone; she had it all and took care of it. Being raised on the ranch, she knew it like the back of her hand.

She often shared with me as she looked back many years to a time and place where, as a young woman, the neighboring ranch boys would come by and call on her, but she was serious with none of them. They were all just friends.

I was thirty-two, and she found me to be an avid hunter, a rambler, a historian, a conversationalist, a raconteur, an adventurer, and most importantly of all, a dear friend.

She was near seventy and was a Hill Country rancher with a 4,000-acre Hereford ranch that had been marked in the state registries as such for almost 135 years.

I was just passing through her world to visit the grandfather of an old Hill Country college friend of mine that in 1968 enlisted and gave his life for his beloved America in Vietnam.

Marjorie was a friend to them and a bordering neighbor who was gracious enough to visit my friend's grave marker with me while walking along the river at twilight and later, allowing me to quail hunt on her land.

We were introduced, and immediately the two of us were drawn to each other. It seemed as if we were two moths drawn to the same flame.

I often pause now and contemplate about it all, and at the time it seemed like I was unexplainably enthralled with her rugged ranch life. I guess she was drawn to my story telling and carefree and wandering mannerisms. I think the real truth was that she just loved cowboys.

After visiting the grave of my old friend, I stood with Marjorie for almost an hour, overlooking the river, as we talked about Tom and his grandfather and how much they had loved each other.

It was dark when Marjorie invited me over to her spread with the promise of plenty of fine quail hunting come morning.

After dinner and a good night's sleep, a great quail hunt was indeed what awaited me. Mid-afternoon, I cleaned birds, and she invited a couple of neighbors for a wonderful fried quail supper.

That is how our friendship started, and from there the story only got better.

How could two individuals meet as ships in the night and by luck find the time and place to share their dreams and thoughts of their futures? This didn't happen just once, but the process was repeated many times over through the years.

These were the kind of things Marjorie and I found time to talk about up on Juniper's Knoll.

She would like to start with, "What's been going on in your world, my friend?"

I would tell her how I had been and how my family was doing and about my wife and kids, about my job as a vocational agriculture teacher and all the judging trips and county fairs and shows that we attended. We sat and talked about livestock and some of the latest breeding trends.

She would sit and smile, occasionally nod her approval, as I would continue on. After a while, it was her turn, and boy could she turn loose with all the ranch activities and talk around the home place.

When she finished, I would look at her and comment, "Marjorie, it does not even seem that I have been gone, my dear."

She would say in return, "Jim, I was thinking the very same thing myself."

We would sit on the Bois d'arc benches, view down the hill across the beautiful landscape that overlooked the Pedernales River. When it was spring, and the wildflowers were blooming, it was such a special kind of "heaven on earth" that we both truly cherished.

The wild turkeys gleaning the hillside were just an added attraction, an addition of aesthetic beauty that no one could ever put a price on or even consider it.

This time was no different than the many times we had spent in the past, just sitting there and visiting. It was during moments such as this that our deepest innermost thoughts would surface, and there was no doubt between us as to how we felt about things that we loved and cared about. No stones went unturned, and we did not hesitate to share them with each other.

One late April afternoon we visited until past dark, and when the sun went down, with us sitting in the dark, it seemed as if more truisms flowed freely from the both of us.

Marjorie was probably the one individual in my life that I could share anything and everything. In return, I think that she felt the same about me.

It was up on that knoll on a bright Sunday morning when she talked about a distant niece in San

Antonio who would inherit her beautiful ranch someday. It would be up to her to carry on the traditions.

Marjorie also shared that the niece was not the least bit interested in the ranch, and it had been thirteen years since she had even been out that way.

Marjorie was looking down the draw as she spoke of these things and when she turned back toward me there was more than just misty eyes that I peered into. After a while I cried along with her, knowing that the end of the story had already been written.

My thoughts often return today to those blessed moments that we shared on Juniper's Knoll and how I wish that I had been financially able to purchase her ranch when she no longer had a need for it.

Had I been able, that is exactly what I would have done to preserve her beloved home and carry her legacy forward a few more years.

Knowing all along that it would be impossible for me to do that saddened me greatly.

When my thoughts occasionally return to Marjorie and her ranch, I cannot help but think of all the good times she graciously shared with me. She didn't have to, she wanted to, and to know my friend was to know why she did it.

I returned several years after Marjorie had passed on and found that her ranch had been sold to real estate developers, and they had divided it up into small ranchettes and had them on the market.

According to the young lady who gave me a tour of the properties, the real estate venture was highly successful, and the city folks were buying up the small tracts just as the developers had planned. Hundreds of thousands of dollars a week were being generated from the sales.

It saddened me greatly when I stopped and looked around. It was evident that the real estate salespeople did not quite understand what I was feeling.

By chance, I was through that part of the country a couple of years ago during an Easter break. It was spring turkey season in the Texas Hill Country once again, and it was not that far out of my way to go by and visit Marjorie's place.

I arrived at the big front entrance of a gated community, and there were BMW's and Cadillac Escalades in abundance, coming and going like it was a freeway.

Not having the combination to enter the big gate, I pulled my old Dodge dually over beside the main entrance and just sat there while thinking about Bob Wills singing *Time Changes Everything*, and thought how indeed, it does.

After a while I exited the truck and made my way through the walk-through and started up the property road. It was about a two mile walk up to Juniper's Knoll, and I was determined to sit on the benches and view those magnificent wildflowers one more time.

After about fifteen minutes, a young facility security guard drove up and commenced to check me out. He asked for identification, and when I opened my wallet he saw my 32 Degree Masonic Lodge membership card that was next to my driver's license.

He, being a Mason himself, began a conversation about my lodge affiliation and what I was doing there on the property.

I told him my story; it was a long sad story, but I told it to him anyway and surprisingly, he looked me in the eye and listened to every word of it.

When I finished, he replied, "Mr. Richardson, those benches are still there today, and I know who owns the tract where they are located. Would you like for me to escort you to that area and allow you to spend some time there?"

I told the youngster that it would make me so happy that I could hug his neck. He laughed and told me to get in his Jeep.

When we arrived at Juniper's Knoll, I do not think I had ever seen the flowers so beautiful. He let me out of the vehicle and told me to go ahead and walk on up to the live oaks while he notified the property owners what we were doing there.

After about an hour, the young man returned and told me that if it was not too much trouble and if I had the time, the owners of the property wanted to meet me and ask questions about my connections with their tract of land.

Gladly, I responded, "It would be my pleasure to meet the Martins and tell my story to them of how I used to spend time up on the knoll with Marjorie and about some of the moments that we shared there."

The next thing I knew we were at their ranch house on the other side of the river, and we were in their living room, overlooking the hillside with all the blooms. The beauty was unexplainable; my love for the place was quite evident.

Looking across the river and the wide draw, I could see our benches in the distance. I pointed them out to Doug and Susie Martin and retraced the path for them that Marjorie and I used to walk along as she fed the wild turkeys, years ago.

In one sense, it seemed as if it was only yesterday that the two of us made the trek.

The two of them had many questions for me, and I had several of the answers to their questions. Our time together flew by, and it was not long until I had been in their home almost three hours.

I finally arose and told them that I must be going, that the visit was wonderful and how much I enjoyed meeting the two of them and spending our time together.

After meeting the Martins, I felt better about what had been troubling me for years. Time does change everything, and we must go on with our lives while being thankful for the ones that we crossed paths with and were momentarily allowed to spend some extra time with them. For all of that, I am truly thankful.

Before leaving the Martins, they told me that they would always welcome me back to their home and that I could come and sit on the benches whenever I felt like I needed to. This made me feel so good.

We exchanged phone numbers, and I thanked the lovely couple and told them that I planned on doing just that and would always be appreciative of the offering they had extended to me.

The last thing that I said to them was, "After meeting the two of you, I know Marjorie is happy now. She knows that a finer couple could not have ended up with her favorite place on this earth."

They smiled at me as I walked out with Gordon. We crawled back in his Jeep, and he drove me to my Dodge dually at the front gate. He gave me his cell phone number and told me that he expected me to call him when I swept back through that country.

I told him that I would be back in Fredericksburg in October for a writers' conference and when I returned I would give him a call.

I shook his hand, got out of his Jeep, and returned to my vehicle. I cranked the engine and took off down the long road leading back to the main highway. I turned west when I got back to the highway and knew that Marjorie was buried only two or three miles down the road in an old cemetery. She was interred there with all of her kin that had gone that way before her.

JIM L. RICHARDSON

Upon arrival, I parked and got out. Her family plot was only a short distance, and upon reaching it I could not help but notice the two beautiful Bois d'arc benches that were placed nearby, on a small knoll, under a couple of small live oaks.

I knew it was Walter's handiwork as I sat down and immediately noticed all of the Texas Bluebonnets and Indian Paintbrushes that were blooming around the plot and in the background. Looking hard, I could see her beautiful river in a distance.

I told Marjorie about her new tenants and how nice they were and how they were preserving the place that she adored. I also told her about how things had changed since she had been gone; there were caretakers looking after her ranch.

Then I thought, Marjorie is not gone, she is just resting there, under the wildflowers and already knows everything that I am telling her.

In a total solemn manner, as I sat there and looked around, I realized then that my friend, Marjorie, was in peace. God bless her dear soul.

The following is not mine and I could not find the author, but I wanted to share it with you. It is very thought provoking.

SHOES IN CHURCH

I showered and shaved............... I adjusted my tie.

I got there and sat............... In a pew, just in time.

Bowing my head in prayer............ As I closed my eyes.

I saw the shoe of the man next to me....... Touching my own. I sighed.

With plenty of room on either side......... I thought, 'Why must our soles touch?'

It bothered me, his shoe touching mine. But it didn't bother him much.

A prayer began: 'Our Father'............ I thought, 'This man with the shoes, has no pride. They're dusty, worn, and scratched. Even worse, there are holes on the side!'

'Thank You for blessings,' the prayer went on.

The shoe man said................ A quiet 'Amen.'

I tried to focus on the prayer....... But my thoughts were on his shoes again.

Aren't we supposed to look our best. When walking through that door?

'Well, this certainly isn't it,' I thought, glancing toward the floor.

Then the prayer was ended............ And the songs of praise began

The shoe man was certainly loud. Sounding proud as he sang.

His voice lifted the rafters. His hands were raised high.

The Lord could surely hear the shoe man's voice from the sky.

It was time for the offering and what I threw in was steep.

I watched as the shoe man reached into his pockets so deep.

I saw what was pulled out, what the shoe man put in.

Then I heard a soft 'clink' as when silver hits tin.

The sermon really bored me to tears, and that's no lie.

It was the same for the shoe man. For tears fell from his eyes.

At the end of the service, as is the custom here.

We must greet new visitors and show them all good cheer.

But I felt moved somehow and wanted to meet the shoe man.

So, after the closing prayer I reached over and shook his hand.

He was old, and his skin was dark, and his hair was truly a mess.

But I thanked him for coming and for being our guest.

He said, 'My name's Charlie. I'm glad to meet you, my friend.'

There were tears in his eyes, but he had a large, wide grin.

'Let me explain,' he said............. Wiping tears from his eyes.

'I've been coming here for months...... And you're the first to say 'Hi."

'I know that my appearance is not like all the rest.

'But I really do try to always look my best.'

'I always clean and polish my shoes, before my very long walk.'

'But by the time I get here, they're dirty and dusty, like chalk.'

My heart filled with pain, and I swallowed to hide my tears.

As he continued to apologize for daring to sit so near

He said, 'When I get here. I know I must look a sight.'

'But I thought if I could touch you. Then maybe our souls might unite.'

I was silent for a moment. Knowing whatever was said

Would pale in comparison. I spoke from my heart, not my head.

'Oh, you've touched me,' I said.......'And taught me, in part'

'That the best of any man. Is what is found in his heart.'

The rest, I thought, this shoe man will never know.

Like just how thankful I really am…that his dirty old shoe touched my soul.

Live each day as your last, for we never know our time here on earth. Love and peace, my friends and remember that it is not how we look on the outside but how we look within.

This concludes, "The Wanderings Of A Traveling Man." Thank you for sharing the journey with me.